The People

how to manage people's

About the Author

Margaret Dale is a Human Resources consultant who has written extensively in the area of people management. She is the co-author of The Business Dimension (Blackhall Publishing).

The People Dimension

how to manage people's performance successfully

Margaret Dale

BLACKHALL
Publishing

This book was typeset by Red Dot for

BLACKHALL PUBLISHING
26 Eustace Street
Dublin 2
Ireland

e-mail: blackhall@tinet.ie

ISBN: 1 901657 57 4

A catalogue record for this book is available from the
British Library.

Printed in Ireland by
Betaprint Ltd

CONTENTS

CHAPTER 6: DEALING WITH ENDINGS AND BEGINNINGS

LIST OF FIGURES

ACKNOWLEDGEMENTS

*My appreciation goes to Helen who helped me recognise
how much my views and approaches have changed as a
result of experience and learning, to Dick who went away
too soon and to Roger for supplying yet more examples and
being so tolerant.*

INTRODUCTION

I used to think that managers deliberately set out to make life hard for the workers. My experience of working alongside managers and being one has taught me that the opposite is sometimes true. But very few workers start out by wanting to make life difficult for their managers – though a few might. For most, something happens to change their view. This may be the unwitting action of the bosses, lessons they learn from their colleagues or something in the culture of the organisation.

I have also learnt that not all managers are evil by design – though I am sure we can all think of some who are. Most try very hard to do a good job but know only one way of managing their staff. They are not aware that other approaches are possible. Regardless of the causes, the results of manager versus worker attitudes combine to result in an unproductive, unhappy and often unsafe workplace.

The attitudes of employees can be influenced by managers who take a different approach and it is possible to change the culture of the workplace. It is possible to transform an inefficient organisation, torn by internal conflict into one where people work profitably together. This book draws on experiences and ideas to help you identify what you may do differently to manage your people more successfully.

1

IN THE BEGINNING

1.1 INTRODUCTION

At the start of a new job, most of us are full of hope, believing it to be the opportunity for success. We begin with the intention of doing a good job and making the most of the chances open to us. As the managers of new members of staff, we prepare for a new starter aware of the risks but believing the best candidate was chosen. We know there will be some challenges but expect the individual will rise to them, do a good job and become a full and productive member of the team, quickly. Existing members of the team may be wary of their new colleague but still look forward to showing them the ropes. There may be the possibility of making a new friend, and perhaps the opportunity to learn from the new employee's experience. Everyone expects, and has no real reason to believe otherwise, that the new working relationship will be longlasting, harmonious and productive.

1.2 IS EVERYBODY HAPPY AT WORK?

Sadly, not everyone is happy at work. It is quite common to hear people complaining about their daily misery. Managers bewail their impossible workload and the poor quality of their staff and decry their peers. It is rare to hear people admit to being happy in their jobs. How many people of your acquaintance say they feel well rewarded, believe they are making a real contribution to their organisation and know where they are going? Even if they say they are, do you believe them? It may be fashionable to describe work in negative terms but it may also be the truth. If the beginning is so full of promise, why does it change?

1.3   WHAT GOES WRONG?

There are lots of reasons why work changes from being a pleasant experience to being an unhappy one. Often at the heart of the problem is the human dimension – the way we behave towards each other and towards ourselves. The dynamics generated in relationships also have an impact. And, as with many other types of relationship, communications (and behind them, mismatched expectations) are frequently the cause of the difficulties.

Some people believe that we are not paid to be happy at work, that all that matters is that employees turn up on time, do their work correctly and do not cause waves. This view is widespread in both management theories and management practice. Some would argue strongly that nothing else is needed to ensure smooth production and bottom line success. Others disagree. Some notable organisations are equally concerned with these measures and take a different approach to managing people's performance. They look at work and the working relationships in their broadest sense and are concerned about the qualitative as well as the contractual aspects of their employees' working life. This approach, they find, has pay-offs in addition to profitability.

1.4   HOW DO YOU MAKE IMPROVEMENTS?

This book aims to explore in practical terms ways in which you can successfully manage people. It is intended to help you and the people you work with realise and profit from these additional benefits. We will look at how some of the human problems grow, how to avoid them and how to deal with them before they get out of hand. But being successful at managing people is not just a case of following the textbooks, copying the actions taken by other organisations, or simply doing more of what worked well in the past. Approaches to people management are evolving as greater insight into the factors that drive us all is gained.

People's expectations of how they should be treated have also altered and continue to change. As people see themselves as full and equal members of a modern consumer society, they demand to be treated as more than just units of production or resources to be harnessed for the well being of their employing organisation. They want a say in things and to be regarded at least as stakeholders, if not partners in the business.

For any manager to be successful at managing people at work, an appreciation of how these differing expectations affect behaviour and attitudes is essential. The manager needs to apply the skills needed to enable people to do their best. In this way staff are allowed to use their knowledge and talents to the best of their abilities. It also means that the problems caused by the need to adapt to new circumstances and change our understanding are reduced. This approach will result in appropriate actions being taken which will also help everyone learn new skills and respond positively to the new situation.

This book will take you through some simple steps that can be taken to create the sort of climate that allows people to learn and work productively together. A manager who is able to create this sort of environment should find that some of the issues that often get in the way of successful performance should not even arise. Those problems that do emerge should be capable of early resolution. Other benefits will also accrue.

For the organisation, this means that:
- mistakes and wastage are reduced;
- customers are given high quality services;
- production of goods or services operate smoothly.

The manager will:
- know that day to day matters are under control;
- have space to plan for the development of the services or operations;
- be able to support personal learning and that of the staff.

The staff will:

- know they are working to their best;
- get the satisfaction of knowing they are doing a good job;
- have the opportunities to develop and improve their skills and abilities.

The starting point for creating this sort of climate is to be clear about the different expectations. If these are set out in the beginning and are openly discussed and reaffirmed continuously, the chances of misunderstandings developing are reduced. We will start by looking at expectations from three perspectives – those of the organisation, the manager and the individual. For together they have a combined effect on performance (see Figure 1.1).

Figure 1.1: Three perspectives on expectations

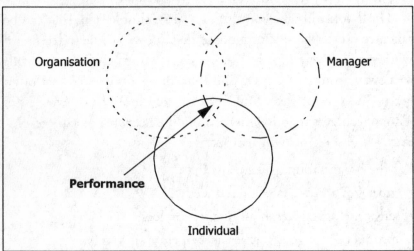

This exploration will give us some insight into how the parties' separate expectations can be clarified and the chances of misconceptions occurring reduced. It will also help us recognise how, if effort is made to align these differing perceptions, performance can be maximised (see Figure 1.2).

Figure 1.2: Aligning expectations

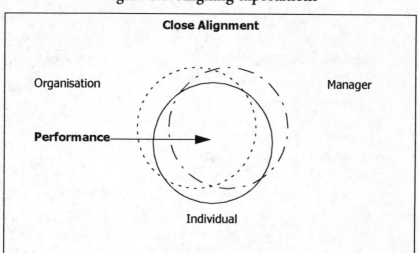

However, if expectations are mismatched or not engaged, performance can be reduced. It is not unknown for individuals to be
disappointed when their expectations are not being met. The
result can be that they have no sense of connection with the
organisation and have a poor relationship with their manager. A
similar situation arises when individuals misunderstand the
objectives of their manager or the organisation.

This kind of situation most often arises when an organisation
is undergoing change. At the beginning of an individual's
employment begins with individual and organisational expectations are closely aligned. The individual initially closely espouses
them, internalising the organisation's value system and hangs on
to them closely although the organisation's mission and circumstances may be altering around them. Eventually the parties find
they have drifted far apart and have very little in common.

Figure 1.3: Mismatched expectations

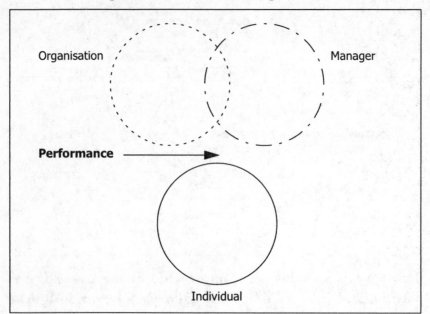

If managers also lose touch with the overall objectives and the expectations of individual employees, the situation becomes totally fragmented. Examples of this can be found in organisations where the employees collectively identify closely with external bodies, such as trade unions or professional groups, and managers are isolated from the organisation as a result of poor communications, highly centralised decision making and rapid change.

Organisation's Expectations

An organisation's expectations are often found in its mission statement (if one exists) or slogans used, for example, in company literature: 'To be the best in a competitive world takes strategic planning and the ability to adapt to ever-changing circumstances.' This suggests that managers and staff are forward looking and able to spot opportunities, prepared to rise to challenges and quick to learn.

The organisation's expectations can also be seen in its definition of its business. For example, in an advertisement, the phrase 'if you see yourself as a salesperson in one of the UK's fastest growth service industries', tells us that customer focus and responsiveness to changing needs will be important in the job.

The organisation's culture will impose expectations, often implicitly, on all its members. The differences between publicly funded and private sector organisations are well known but even organisations in the same sector display different types of assumptions, standards and expectations of types of behaviour and attitude. For example, Lloyds Bank and the Halifax are both in the financial sector but they present themselves publicly as very different kinds of bank. The differences are not only found in the sorts of services provided to customers. The way each organisation presents itself as an employer and the ways in which it treats its staff vary.

Department's Expectations

The purpose and function of a department or section affect the behaviour and performance of the people working in it. For example, a finance department has a different approach and expects different patterns of behaviour from its staff than the marketing department. These differences are due to the nature of the work and the sort of person attracted to work in those functions. The finance department, by its very nature, tends to focus on the needs of the organisation and most of its customers are within the organisation. It also looks back to what has happened in the past. The marketing department, on the other hand, looks outwards at customers and the actions of competitors. Its role is to anticipate future trends and opportunities.

The key objectives of the department or section also dictate expectations and influence performance. For example, if the objectives are clearly expressed, and all staff are signed up to them, there is a good chance that the efforts of the team will be geared, jointly, towards their achievement. If, however, the objectives are confused, contradictory and changing, the chances are that the team will reflect these conditions and will not work well together. Individuals will do what they think is expected of them. They may spend a lot of their time disagreeing with their colleagues, and possibly with their manager, about who should be doing what when and why rather than working on what really matters. Imagine the effect if Figure 1.1 was multiplied by the number of different individuals in the section (see Figure 1.4).

Figure 1.4: Confused Expectations

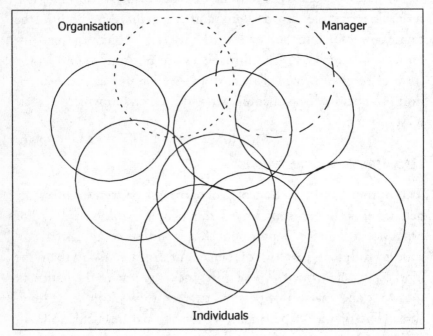

In Figure 1.4 where does the performance arrow go? The picture appears and is, no doubt, chaotic.

The relationships developed with other departments, suppliers and customers also influence what staff believe is expected of them. Furthermore, these affect the standards to which they perform. For example, in an organisation that encourages internal competition, the winning of the competition can take over from achieving the organisation's overall objectives. This effect is often seen in companies that are divided into areas with great emphasis placed on the achievement of sales targets. This can result in separate areas stealing customers from each other rather than putting effort into increasing the company's overall share of the market.

The standards expected by customers can also skew staff's attention away from the organisation's objectives. For example, in a highly devolved company, it is possible that a manager puts too much effort into safeguarding a single but valued customer. This could perhaps result in too much discount being offered simply to steal the march on a competitor in one deal rather than assess the true value of the customer to the company. Trying to help suppliers can also distort expectations away from the real purpose.

Manager's Expectations

The manager's personal style and interpretation of expectations inevitably has a large influence on the understanding of staff and their own expectations. The way in which managers approach the role and tasks of managing the work of other people, and the particular function or project for which they have responsibility, is influenced and affected by a number of factors, not least the personality of the individual concerned. Some of these are illustrated in Figure 1.5.

Figure 1.5: Factors affecting a manger's style

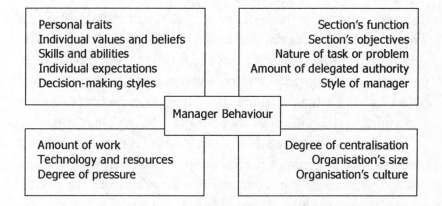

The top left-hand box in Figure 1.5 represents those factors intrinsic to the individual. To a certain extent these can be directly controlled by the individual. Developing the skills and abilities to do this is a central responsibility for all managers. It is also possible to develop or change your decision-making style, if the one you are using is proving to be ineffective. Questioning value systems and attitudes and exploring the realism of expectations can be covered in some management development programmes. Changing personality is more difficult, but behaviour can be altered. However, the degree of behaviour change is often conditioned by the factors outside the individual manager's control.

The top right-hand box contains factors which can be influenced, in part, by the manager. The way in which the work is organised and allocated and similarly the way in which staff are developed depends on the manager. The way in which the tasks and problems are viewed in addition to the ways they are addressed will also reflect the manager's attitudes. Some managers see a challenge in a negative light. For others it is an opportunity to rise to and may provide the chance of learning and developing new skills.

The authority vested in a manager varies, and not only according to the organisation's policies and practices. It reflects the degree of trust in and the esteem accorded to the manager. This grows over the time the manager is in position and reflects the impression created (possibly falsely) by past successes and failures. The relationship between the manager and the manager's manager is part of this and influences the former's ability to act independently. It also governs the assessment of what can and cannot be achieved. Thus are formed the manager's expectations (hopes and aspirations) and in turn those of the staff in the section.

The bottom left-hand box contains variable factors that are products of the needs of the moment. The pressure on the section, the nature of the work and the availability of the needed resources, separately and combined, influence the expectations and behaviour of the people working there. A busy section, under pressure to achieve exacting targets, finds that everyone's expectations and daily routines are highly constrained. The scope for action is determined by the needs of the moment and the time horizons are short.

The nature of the technology, whether it helps to do the work and how effectively the staff are able to use it, dictate what is possible and what everyone expects to get from their job. Take, for example, a section where staff are working with computer equipment which is operating at its limits but they do not know how to deal with its glitches. They are more likely to focus on making sure the system does not crash rather than on providing up to date management information. Contrast this with the section fully equipped with up to date systems operated by trained and competent staff. They will be able to concentrate on achieving objectives which move their business forward. However, getting hold of such resources does not depend simply on the section's manager's abilities to access them; the demands and needs of other sections within the organisation and the availability of funds also play a part.

The pressure felt by the staff in the section is, again, a product of a number of factors. These include their work, the way the manager and staff jointly and separately respond to the demands made on them and the culture of the organisation. Some managers panic; others respond calmly to whatever unforeseen event arises. Their response affects the expectations of everyone else involved in the immediate work environment.

The bottom right-hand box represents the organisational factors that have an impact on the manager's behaviour and constrain managerial actions. Even in the most liberal, highly decentralised organisation, a manager is under pressure to conform to the organisation's normal methods of working. Some organisations seem to generate a sense of chaos and impending doom from the smallest unforeseen occurrence; others take such incidents in their stride. One feature that differentiates the chaotic from the organised is the quality of the planning. If good plans, containing contingencies, have been drawn up, they will provide for such eventualities.

To be successful at managing people, you need to be aware of how these different factors combine to influence your behaviour. You need to know which of these lie within your control and which are beyond it. This assessment should be realistic as it is not uncommon for managers to believe they are not able to influence a situation or control certain factors when, in fact, all that is needed to do so is self-confidence and courage. The pay-off for taking the risk can be well worth the investment. We will discuss later how, even if one of the factors is really beyond your influence, it is possible to deal with it and minimise any negative effects.

In the following chapters, we will discuss how the manager can achieve the twin goals of being in control and successfully managing people. We will start by exploring how to clarify different expectations. For, unless these are made explicit, it will not be possible to set standards of performance. It may seem obvious to say this but it is important. Unless the required levels of performance are understood, it will not be possible to know if they are being achieved and maintained. It will not be possible to exceed them, nor will it be possible to take early action to stop things going wrong.

Monitoring performance can be used to prevent staff from acting on their initiative and following personal flights of fancy. Alternatively, it can be used to provide rapid feedback so that if any remedial action is required it can be taken early. It is equally important that everyone can see what works well. Once you have identified which aspects of performance need to be monitored you will be able to devise useful systems to provide the right information and enable feedback to come from appropriate sources.

We will discuss how to do this and consider how best to manage the people who do not conform to the expected patterns of performance. We will also examine how standards can be used as a platform for development. They can be used to identify the areas of perceived weakness in need of strengthening. Additionally, any negative impact can be reduced. Standards can also be used to identify strengths that may previously have been unrecognised – as unused strengths tend to decay. Using standards can help to ensure that individuals and managers are aware of one another's potential and know how to play to their collective strengths.

Even when standards have been well set and everyone is clear about their own expectations, those required for the achievement of their collective objectives and the organisation's goals, things can go wrong. Most often this happens as a result of changes in the environment in which they are operating. Typically, change creeps up on people and can take everyone by surprise. Planning and environmental scanning can help prevent this. But inevitably, change will occur at some point. It is the responsibility of all managers to ensure that everyone, themselves included, is able to respond positively and deal effectively with those changes. These words are often said, but to manage the environment and people really well, a manager needs to appreciate what may be happening to those people.

All good things come to an end. Life is not simply a matter of beginnings and middles. Changes to organisations, situations and individual circumstances can, for one reason or another, end working partnerships. Well-known working practices have to be changed from time to time. Deeply held value systems, when opened for scrutiny, can be found to be no longer appropriate. Belief systems need to be examined and re-framed in the light of new insights. Although they may take us by surprise, most endings are predictable.

With thought and understanding, a manager can prepare for most endings and be ready to help the team respond positively to what is in effect a bereavement. Introducing new people into a well-established work team can also be a challenge for a manager.

Naturally, existing staff are wary of a new person. They have to get to know each other and gain an understanding of their respective expectations. The role of the manager in establishing the right sort of climate for the generation of new relationships can be central to the long-term functioning of the new team.

Another new beginning is the application of new learning. We have already discussed how personal style can affect the way in which a manager manages. The final chapter will examine in more detail ways in which you can change your performance as a manager. We all know that it is not possible to go on a course, learn all about how to manage people and start to do it successfully the next day. It is not as easy as that. People are far more complicated and unpredictable than the simple lessons taught on short courses make out. Time and practice are needed to build and refine skills. The people being managed also need to be prepared to allow their manager to change. We are often trapped in our histories. So breaking out of the past and beginning again can be difficult. However, it is not possible for anyone, manager or staff, who wants to apply new skills and behaviour patterns, to escape this phase.

2

STANDARDS AND OBJECTIVES

2.1 INTRODUCTION

Setting standards involves more than defining and agreeing business objectives. Objectives are about targets and end results; standards describe the means used to achieve those ends. They are also indicators of the attitudes and expectations underpinning an organisation. If these are not made explicit and understood by all concerned, it is possible to find that although superb results may have been obtained, the way they were achieved was not 'the way we do things around here'. The sad story of Nick Leeson and the Barings Bank illustrates what can happen when someone, left to get on with things, does just that. When things start to go wrong, there is no way back into the organisation to call on support or alert the people who need to know.

A culture which allows people to blame one another is neither forward looking nor healthy. Such an organisation may purport to allocate responsibility and give staff authority for getting things done. The reality is often different. Employees may be given responsibility but not the authority they need. They might be told about their objectives but the standards of performance expected may not be clear. Even when these standards have been outlined, they may well be changed. It is not unusual for people to be held to account for events outside their control. The result is that their self-confidence is undermined and their efforts are dismissed. The focus, in this sort of climate, is retrograde and when things go wrong, there are few opportunities to wonder what you have learnt from an episode, how to put matters right, and how to prevent it happening again.

A different type of climate can be developed. If you use a robust and participative approach to setting and agreeing objectives and standards; you can avoid creating such a negative environment. You will be able to create an open organisation, i.e. one that enables individuals to be involved in management processes and participate in decisions that affect them and their work. In this type of culture mistakes are seen as opportunities for learning rather than being examples of failure. In this sort of climate, it is possible to build higher levels of performance, meet people's expectations and sustain long-term organisational achievement.

2.2   OBJECTIVES

Peter Drucker,[1] one of the first management gurus tells us:

> *If objectives are only good intentions they are worthless. They must degenerate into work. And work is always specific, always has, or should have, unambiguous, measurable results, a deadline and a specific assignment of responsibility.*

Objectives are often confused with aims and goals. Aims are broad areas of intent; goals are to be aimed at. Objectives outline the steps that need to be taken to achieve the organisation's goals and make its mission a reality. Objectives, as Drucker intimated, should:

1. **Contain precise, clearly defined actions.** These should be written in plain English, contain active verbs and specify the required outcome.
2. **Be self-contained.** Each objective statement should stand on its own and be easy to communicate to all those who need to understand what is to be achieved. For example, telling the sales staff to increase the size of the customer base warns them that they need to find more new customers, keep existing ones and win back those who may be considering changing supplier.

---

1. Drucker, *The Practice of Management* (1955).

3. **Be owned.** The people responsible for taking the actions should be identified and given access to both the resources and the authority they need to achieve the objectives successfully. Thus the example above becomes: all sales staff will increase the overall number of 'live' customers by finding new ones, retaining existing ones and winning back those lost to other suppliers.

4. **Have deadlines.** The timescales should be achievable and contain contingencies for the unexpected problems, for they always arise. Review periods should be in-built so that progress can be assessed and remedial action can be taken early. The example thus becomes: all sales staff will, during the next financial year, increase the overall number of 'live' customers by finding new ones, retaining existing ones and winning back those recently lost to other suppliers. Bi-monthly reviews of progress will take place.

5. **Have milestones so that progress can be assessed.** Thus all sales staff will, during the next financial year, increase the overall number of 'live' customers by 15 per cent. This will occur as a result of finding new customers, retaining existing ones and winning back those lost to other suppliers. Bi-monthly reviews of progress will take place to ensure that the overall trend is upwards. It is expected that the customer base will have increased by 3 per cent after three months, 8 per cent after six months and 12.5 per cent after nine months.

2.3 STANDARDS

Standards are the patterns and levels of behaviour required to achieve the objectives, they can also be termed competencies. As we have already said they are often ignored or the need for their specification goes unrecognised. Attention is more often given to the ends rather than the means. Yet it is often the means that affect long-term success.

If we take the above objective and develop the example, we can see that the short-term objective of achieving the required increase in customers can be attained in a number of ways. These can include, for example:

(a) engaging in high-profile marketing;

(b) undercutting competitors;

(c) giving repeat business customers generous discounts;

(d) undermining the credibility and reputation of competitors' products;

(e) wining and dining lost customers;

(f) paying attention to the quality of service and ensuring delivery of products is timely and correct;

(g) keeping in touch with distribution so that customers can be alerted to any problems at an early stage;

(h) talking to customers to find out what they want;

(i) contacting potential customers and asking what they would like to see;

(j) making sure product development and production are aware of customers' changing requirements;

(k) making sure the price/quality ratio is correct, according to the customers' definition;

(l) contacting lost customers to find out why they changed, dealing, where possible, with the source of their dissatisfaction and then telling them what has been done;

(m) investigating what competitors are doing to develop their products and services;

(n) feeding 'intelligence' back into the organisation to help develop the future plans.

Which do you think will help grow the customer base and contribute to long-term success?

Specifying standards of performance directs attention to the 'what and how' and allows focused remedial action to be taken as soon as it looks as though things may be going awry. If performance is slipping, it is possible that the individual responsible is not achieving their objectives because they:

(a) do not know how to do what is expected;

(b) do not understand what is expected;

(c) misunderstood what is expected;

(d) had mixed (and wrong) priorities;

(e) they chose to do something different.

The first two points require action to skill up the individual and deal with the factors that are blocking their comprehension. The third requires clarification and examination of why the misunderstanding arose in the first place to ensure it does not happen again. The fourth requires the refocusing of effort and appreciation of why the priorities were different. It is possible that the individual was receiving mixed messages or was under pressure from someone else to act in ways other than those required. Only the fifth example may require disciplinary action at an early stage.

Discipline does not necessarily imply punishment, although there are occasions when this may be the best course of action to take. Frequently, we are too quick to hand out rebukes and reprimands. We need someone to blame and finding fault is easier than taking the time to understand what led to the substandard performance.

'Discipline' is an interesting word. Its meanings range from control and order using a system of rule to maintain behaviour to mental, moral or physical training, or a brand of instruction or learning, or punishment. Its root is in 'disciple', a follower or pupil of a leader, teacher, philosophy. Thus defined fully, discipline can be regarded more as teaching people the 'right' way to behave and establishing what is 'wrong' according to a set of shared principles or codes.

Using standards to guide behaviour and develop performance does not necessarily mean that you need to be a strict authoritarian. It does, however, require clarity about the standards expected and what they mean to those directly affected by them. As organisations get bigger, and become more dispersed and decentralised, more responsibility is delegated to managers. Regardless of whether this was a result of a conscious decision or happened as a product of growth, the organisation needs to have what Peters and Waterman[2] called "simultaneous loose-tight properties". They found that:

> *Autonomy is a product of discipline. The discipline (a few shared values) provides the framework. It gives people confidence (to experience for instance) stemming from stable expectations about what really counts.*

The framework contains the standards.

The example developed above can be used to show how the sales team can take advantage of the slope of the growth curve. If they take the first three months to do the ground work and develop their approach to their customers, it is possible that they would achieve and possibly exceed their annual objective. The team that rushed out to get the easy targets using quick-fix methods could well find itself struggling to get those customers who were not such a soft touch.

2.4 HOW TO SET OBJECTIVES

Objectives are drawn from the organisation's strategic or business plan. This outlines how the organisation will focus its energies, deploy its resources and change its activities to remain in existence and achieve its reason for existing. (This could alternatively be called the mission, primary or core purpose or vision.)

The objectives can be developed as:

(a) a rational process by senior managers and/or planners who compare where the organisation is now in relation to where it

---

2. Peters & Waterman, *In Search of Excellence: Lessons from America's Best-run Companies* (1982).

wants to be. The gap identifies the steps needed to realise the organisation's ambition. Various techniques, such as scenario planning, strategic analysis, environmental scanning and benchmarking, are used to identify what needs to be done. This approach can result in revolution. If the organisation decides to head off in a totally new direction, the degree of change needed could be quite dramatic and could require staff to act in totally different ways and meet new standards of performance;

(b) an evolutionary process building on what the organisation has done before. The change curve tends to be smoother but can be so smooth that nothing alters;

(c) a result of a systematic analysis of the organisation's current performance and the identification of strengths and weaknesses against key measures. These can be compared to the organisation's purpose and appropriate actions identified to change those not meeting the required standards. The objectives will specify which operations need to be changed, those to be maintained, those which need to be stopped and any new ones to be started. This approach can be *both* revolutionary *and* evolutionary.

Objectives need to be:

- **Developmental**. Identifying areas to be grown from existing activities.
- **Change-focused**. Identifying new areas to be introduced or those to be stopped.
- **Maintaining**. Identifying areas which are to be continued, unchanged, at the same standards of performance.
- **Individual**. Identifying those to be achieved by one person or a number of individuals acting alone.
- **Shared**. Identifying those shared by a team or the whole organisation.

- **Task-focused**. Identifying those relating to an area of work, technology or practice.
- **Personal**. Identifying those relating to the skills and relationships of the people in the organisation.

Regardless of their focus, objectives, according to Drucker, should always result in work. This means they should be:

- *Specific*. They should be in words that everyone can understand and precise in their meaning.
- *Measurable*. It should be possible to assess progress in tangible terms. You should know how well you are doing.
- *Achievable*. The objectives and standards should be capable of being attained by a normal competent member of staff, but they should not be easy. They should contain elements of challenge and require the individuals to stretch themselves. If they are too easy, people become complacent and then standards and effort tend to slip. If they are too difficult, they could result in complete disaffection.
- *Relevant*. They should relate directly to the work of the individuals involved and clearly link the objectives of the section and those of the whole organisation. For example improving the level of customer service may seem irrelevant to a section without contact with the organisation's customers unless the links and contribution they make to overall customer service are clearly spelled out.
- *Timed*. Objectives need to have timescales attached so that it is possible to set priorities and assess progress. Standards should be periodically reviewed to ensure they remain achievable and relevant.

For example a set of *SMART* objectives for a company supplying business support services could be, in the next twelve months:

(a) 70 per cent of queries are to result in orders;

(b) 75 per cent of orders are to be repeats;

(c) invoices unpaid after 90 days are to be reduced to 2 per cent;

(d) new business opportunities are to be investigated and at least two new services are to be developed and implemented.

These objectives have implications for the standards of performance of all staff. The first, for example, requires all sales staff and others responding to queries of any kind, even the reception staff, to have obligations to deal with those queries in ways which engage the enquirer and lead to a business transaction.

Similarly, the second requires the customer to be so satisfied that they return for more.

The third objective has implications for accounts staff as well as those dealing directly with the customer. Those in direct contact need to know their customers and be able to deal with them in a way that ensures payments are made in line with the agreed time period. The staff dealing with customers who do not meet their obligations are required to act in such a way that secures payment *and* retains the business of the customer so that the second objective is not compromised.

The final objective expects all staff to listen to what their customers are saying about their wants and future possible requirements and to feed those comments into the company. It also requires them to understand the whole of the business, not just their section, and to think about how to improve their areas of work for the benefit of the whole.

It is easy for an organisation to set down grand business objectives and expect certain standards of performance from its staff. However, unless the people affected understand objectives and appreciate what the standards mean for their own performance, they will be merely words on paper, unworthy of the trees sacrificed for their display. People need to be involved in the setting of objectives and the specification of standards, if they are to work wholeheartedly for their attainment.

2.5   HOW TO SPECIFY STANDARDS

Standards represent the behaviours required for effective performance. They also reflect the organisation's underpinning value systems. The values may be explicit, contained in documents such as
rules, regulations and procedures. They can also be implicit – this
is the way we do things around here. 'Our way' is taught to new
people during their induction period, be this a planned, formal
occasion or informal, i.e. just allowed to happen. Informal induction can also be called socialisation or conditioning.

Any form of group, work-based or social, takes action to
ensure that a new member understands and eventually conforms
to its accepted patterns and standards of behaviour. Demonstration of the preferred behaviour is rewarded, in ways that range
from the subtle to the directly obvious. Examples include being
allowed to join the tea club, being asked to join the 'group' for a
drink after work, being thanked publicly by a senior manager.
Similar action is taken to rebuke an individual who is not con-
forming. Exclusion or public ridicule are not uncommon methods used by groups to bring about compliance to group norms.
The Hawthorne Experience[3] was perhaps the most famous
research study into how group behaviour can influence performance of individuals and a work group.

When individuals do not make the mark or refuse to conform,
often they are rejected – some sooner than others. Some employers use probationary periods to formalise this process. For example, a new member of staff is allowed between six months and one
year to learn the ropes and fit in with their new employer's expectations. If they do not meet the standard expected of them, their
contract of employment can be terminated with no redress available. Good employers provide special assistance to the new starters
during this period and formalise the induction process. A com-

---

3. The Hawthorne Experiment is described in Handy, *Understanding Or-
    ganisations* (1985).

mon approach to the induction programme includes off-the-job sessions designed to provide the information new staff need and initial job-related training to ensure they have the basic skills. Other actions include buddying and mentor schemes. A buddy is a more experienced work colleague who sometimes has been trained as a job trainer. A mentor is typically an experienced and senior employee who also acts as a role model. As well as demonstrating preferred patterns of behaviour for the new starters to copy, the buddy and the mentor can give advice and tips on how to fit in and make progress in the organisation.

By now you might have guessed that the standards of an organisation reflect its culture and are built up over a period of years. If this is the only way they have been established, it can be quite difficult to make them explicit enough to pass on to others without relying exclusively on hidden messages and hints. If the induction is purely based on socialisation, it can be very difficult for new people to find out what they have to do to succeed. If you find that you are recruiting a lot of people who do not stay very long, you might check to see if they are being expected to meet standards which they do not properly understand.

If you find that this, or something similar, is happening, it may be worth bringing the standards into the open. As well as addressing the immediate problem, you will be able to see if the standards are contributing to achieving the organisation's objectives. Some may, in fact, be counter-productive or perhaps set too high. Excessively high standards can be found in organisations where meticulous and laborious ways of working are too costly.

For example, a restaurant prided itself on the amount of attention it gave to each customer. Each diner was made to feel as though there was no one else in the dining room. However, the restaurant began to lose business as other restaurants became more fashionable and tastes changed. The management team decided that drastic action was needed. The restaurant was refurbished and a new menu introduced. The re-launch was hugely successful and the dining room was full from Monday to Saturday; but the waiting staff were not happy. Although they were still expected to make the customers feel special, they had been told that they should no longer attend closely to their every whim and meet their every need. Comments showed that the customers were more than happy with the level of service – but the staff believed that standards were dropping.

To make sure staff know what is expected of them and to ensure those standards complement the organisation's objectives they need to be:

1. **In the open and shared**. This means that staff are told about the standards and understand what they mean to them in practice.

2. **Specific and simple**. Each standard should only concern one area of behaviour or skill. Mixed standards or ones that are expressed in vague terms should be avoided.

3. **Expressed in behavioural terms so they can be described in detail and demonstrated**. Staff may need to be shown what to do to meet the standards and have a go themselves. Remember the maxim: 'I hear and I forget, I see and I remember, I do and I understand.'

4. **Practical and take account of everyday working realities**. There is little point in having standards that are irrelevant to the current context of the organisation or are not within range of the staff concerned.

The importance of involving staff can not be overestimated. Having their active and willing participation is essential if you expect them to work towards achieving the standards and adopt them as their normal patterns of behaviour. A visit to a McDonald's restaurant will give you an opportunity to watch a number of people working to another's standard of behaviour. If you have the chance to visit several restaurants in different cities, or even in different countries, reflect on how the multinational chain is able to assure such high levels of conformity. How do you think they manage it?

The company is able to achieve this because it has highly focused training and uses a detailed staff manual. This lays down in precise terms what to do and say, and when. You can define the behaviour of a 'good' member of staff by using a technique described by Robert Mager.[4] He suggests that you ask yourself: How will I know one when I see one? Then use the following steps to identify the standards of behaviour required.

1. Write down the goal describing a required outcome.
2. Write down the things you would want someone to say or do to cause you to agree that they have achieved the goal.
3. How do I know one?
4. What do I want one to do?
5. What do I want one not to do?

Sort out step (2), delete any duplications and unwanted items. Repeat (1) and (2) for any remaining aspects of performance considered important. Make coherent, complete statements to describe what you intend for each of the performances on the list. Describe the nature, quality or amount you consider acceptable. Test the statements with the question: If someone achieved or demonstrated each of the standards, would I be willing to say they have achieved it?

In the case of the waiter in the re-launched restaurant, you can ask: What do I expect a good waiter to do? Following Mager's guidance we would say that a good waiter makes sure the diner is satisfied.

Then identify a number of statements to describe what the waiter would do to satisfy the diner. For example:

1. A good waiter checks a few minutes after serving each course to make sure that everything is to the diner's satisfaction.
2. If so, the waiter leaves the diner to eat undisturbed unless called to return.

---

4. Mager, *Goal Analysis* (1984).

3. If not, the waiter takes appropriate action to deal with the cause of the dissatisfaction.

4. A good waiter does not hover at a diner's elbow throughout the meal.

Who defines the statements is for you to decide. As with setting objectives, your circumstances dictate the degree of participation possible. McDonald's did not consult all its employees when laying down the standards of performance. The standards would have been carefully defined to link tightly to the organisation's core business and objectives. In a different type of organisation it may be possible to achieve more involvement from those required to attain the standards. The situation also has an effect. For example, if the conditions are highly uncertain and changing, the participation of all or most of those affected in setting the standards will lead to the levels of commitment needed to attain them. Alternatively, in an organisation with a different culture such a participative approach could be seen by the staff as an indication of weakness. Making those decisions and getting them right tests leadership skills and judgement.

2.6   THE IMPORTANCE OF INVOLVING PEOPLE

We have already mentioned the need for staff to be committed to meeting the standards expected of them and having a sense of ownership of the objectives. This is easily said. It is more difficult putting it into practice. Most of us at some time have felt disappointed and let down by our staff when they failed to achieve what they were meant to achieve, when they did not behave in an acceptable fashion or let the side down. The question often arises of how one manager, alone, in a large organisation can ensure that everyone understands what is expected of them all the time. Even more to the point, how can the one manager ensure that all the staff agree, are committed to shared objectives and act according to the organisation's standards?

Before we discuss the how and when of involving people let us first look at what can happen if people are not committed to the organisation's standards and objectives. We have already referred to the Baring case. This may seem to be an extreme example, a product of the high-flying 1980s. But this sort of situation is not confined to the realms of big business. It can happen in any size of organisation, at any time.

What happens when Things go Wrong?

Let's take the case of a new branch. A keen, young manager thought she had done everything right. She had spent time in the first few weeks, talking to her team. She had made sure that they got to know one other well and understood the different roles each was to play. Her role as manager was to run and develop the business, talk to existing customers and find new ones. Peter, one of the two sales staff, was to run the internal side, making sure that procedures were set in place and dealing with customers' queries and repeat orders. Katrina's job was to run the administration side. She was to order goods, keep stock records and send out accounts. Michael covered external sales. His job was to spend most of his time on the road, selling products and goods. The manager explained their priorities carefully. They were to establish themselves as the major distributor of their product. As they could not compete on price, they would have to be the best on delivery time, quality of customer care and overall efficiency. The team did well for their first nine months and exceeded their targets.

The manager was pleased and started to look to the long-term future. She felt computers would be the way of building their business. She gained the agreement of the company's managing director and spent a small fortune on state-of-the-art equipment. It took quite a while for the manager to get used to the new programs. The rest of the staff noticed the days slipping by as she spent more and more time in the office and less and less visiting customers. Meanwhile Katrina was struggling. She was not very confident with computers and some of the programs installed on the new system completely confused her. She found the best way was to keep her paper records up to date while the manager played with the new IT ones. Nevertheless, she found that things were becoming out of date and the two sets of records did not tie together. Stock items were being used without replacements being ordered and agreements reached with customers were not being recorded. Sometimes invoices were sent out containing mistakes and there had been a few embarrassing occasions when promised deliveries had not been made at all.

Meanwhile, Michael was having a wonderful time. He was out of the office most days and revelling in the freedom he was allowed. Before joining this employer, he had worked for a company whose philosophy had been 'stock em high, sell em cheap'. He found that this approach paid off wonderfully well and he had been able to do several really good deals that undercut his competitors. Peter, however, was growing more and more frustrated. Michael was not checking the availability or price of products and he was increasingly having to go back to customers to explain that delivery times would be longer and prices would be different to those promised. Peter decided that Michael was incompetent. As he was getting fed up with apologising for his colleague's mistakes, he began to tell customers what he thought so that it would not reflect on him.

What had gone wrong with the team that had worked so well? It is easy to see the mistakes when looking at the narrative of a very common scenario. The stated standards and business objectives had been high-jacked by a computer. The first big mistake the manager had made was not to involve the staff, especially Katrina, in the decision to use IT.

The manager had allowed herself to become absorbed in the new toy and involved in the detail. The result was the neglect of her real job. She had taken her eye off the ball as the seductive power of the computer won her attention. Her focus was taken away from the business and the satisfaction of her customers' needs. Her staff followed her example.

1. Katrina had not been involved in the development of the new systems and therefore had not been prepared to learn how to use them. She was isolated from the new technology and so was not able to learn how to use the new programs. By maintaining the paper systems, she was not moving forward.

2. The manager's involvement in detail and the development of two parallel systems led to mistakes that had a direct impact on the customer. Time was being wasted and the company was demonstrating its internal problems to the outside world.

3. Michael, being left to his own devices, was doing his own thing and had reverted to previous standards. The communication between the team and their shared understanding was being eroded by neglect. Instead of working together, he and Peter were worked against each other.

4. Without the co-ordination from their manager, communications and team spirit between her and the rest of the team were falling apart. It is not surprising that Peter adopted the 'watch my back' approach.

Without clear standards and agreed objectives, internal warfare can take energy away from the business. Instead of talking about operational matters, staff begin to complain and moan. Their negative vibes can be felt by the customers, even when staff try to put a brave face on matters. More importantly, it is not long before mistakes start to impact directly on customers. Symptoms of things going wrong include duplication of effort, wrong information, changing details (for example, regarding product availability and prices of stock and services), unmet delivery times, confusion from staff and a sense of dissatisfaction all round. It is not surprising that when customers begin to detect these features of disorganisation, they move their business to other companies.

What happens when Things go Right?

The above example can be used to show how, if the manager had taken a different approach from the very beginning, an upward spiral instead of a decline, could have been achieved. If Katrina had been given responsibility for the system, the manager would have been able to concentrate on the customers, keep Michael on track and the team together.

A team working well is one that has shared objectives and common agreement on standards. This is achieved and maintained through regular discussion and debate in which everyone is involved. The regular discussion may seem to be a luxury and a waste of time. However, if understanding is not checked and the standards reaffirmed, over time people will gradually develop their own interpretations and drift from the initial understanding.

Keeping everyone working on the same priorities reduces the scope for internal conflict and competition. Their energy will be devoted to doing the job instead of arguing among themselves. They will not waste time correcting mistakes and apologising to customers, dealing with complaints, repeating work or finding new customers to replace those lost as a result of poor service. As everyone is focused on what is important, they will be in tune with each other and the needs of the business. They know what they and the others are doing, and because they all know who is responsible for what, they will not duplicate another's efforts, or step on toes, and will be able to recognise and cover gaps. The reduction in mistakes and wasted energy, and the avoidance of duplication will release time. This can be used to improve working practices, develop skills and learn the new ones needed to keep abreast of changing situations.

There is no easy way to achieve this harmony. So much of getting it right depends on the combination of the situation, the circumstances and how the people meld together. You will need to use your leadership skills and judgement to decide which is the best way for your situation and people. A few guiding principles will help you avoid the pitfalls. Once you have assessed your situation, the first and possibly the most important decision is decide who to involve, and when to involve them. Involvement does not guarantee that each person's performance will always meet the standards or be focused on the business objectives. But appropriate participation will help to reduce the chances of these not being achieved.

To Involve or not to Involve?

Sometimes it is more appropriate to impose objectives and standards. Those critical to organisational success or failure or those fundamental to the nature of the business should be non-negotiable. However, they do not need to be imposed rigidly. Even if the standard is non-debatable, effort can be made to explain the reasons for this, the implications of the standard and to ensure that all members of staff understand what they will mean in practice to them. The importance of good quality communications will be repeated many times.

There are occasions when a participative approach can be the wrong one or needs to be hedged with caution. Involvement does not mean asking everyone for their opinion on everything all of the time. Excessive involvement is not democratic, nor is it a managed approach, it is anarchy – and anarchy, being a lack of order, usually results in chaos.

People tend not to be very happy in chaotic situations. They become stressed and unsure. They do not know whether their labours will result in success or failure and tend to put more effort into minding their own backs than doing their job. Inevitably, levels of care, attention and productivity, even attendance, fall.

On the other hand, even when the objectives and standards are vital for organisational success, their importance should not necessarily exclude staff from the process of setting them. It simply means that their involvement should be appropriate and designed to achieve the following:

1. **Understanding.** The practical meaning of the objectives and standards and the reasons behind their establishment.

2. **Acceptance.** The readiness to concur with something even if total agreement has not been attained. If people comprehend the underpinning philosophy, and feel that they have contributed to its development, they are likely to be more committed than if they cannot see the logic, or feel that their opinions are not valued or wanted.

3. **Ownership.** Without their involvement and acceptance of the objectives and standards, staff will not make more than the minimum effort required of them. If their understanding and acceptance have been obtained, it is more likely that they will feel a sense of responsibility for achievement. They will be more inclined to make the extra effort that moves the organisation from being ordinary to being better than the rest.

Figure 2.1 will help you decide which level of involvement is the most appropriate for the situation. It is based on the C:E ratio.

Figure 2.1: Matrix for determining the appropriate level of involvement

	Enforcement	
Conformity	*High*	*Low*
High	Strong Imposition	High Involvement
Low	Police State	Anarchy

1. If you need high levels of conformity and commitment and have the power to enforce compliance, it does not really matter whether you involve your staff or not. You will be able to ensure they work to the standards and attain the objectives through systems of rewards and punishment.

2. High levels of conformity will attract high levels of praise and reward (often in the form of bonus, performance-related pay and the like).

3. Low conformity will attract punishment, often in the form of blame, ridicule, social exclusion, punishment, disciplinary action or even dismissal.

4. If you have a lot of power but no sense of direction, you will end up with the equivalent of a police state. People will do what they have to do. They will not do what they are forbidden to do because they will want to avoid punishment, but they will not have any sense of commitment to the organisation unless they are part of it. Rebellion will be close to the surface. Maintenance of order will depend totally on keeping hold of the power and resources needed to control those who do not agree.

An organisation that has no power to enforce its basic mores and has no common purpose to provide a bond for its members fails to fulfil the very definition of an organisation. The eventual result will either be disintegration or anarchy.

If you need high commitment but do not have the power to enforce conformity, you must seek ownership of the organisation's objectives and standards. This is most often and most easily gained through involvement.

Who to Involve

Deciding who to involve and when to involve them requires skills and is often a test of your abilities. Sales targets may be met and the budget well under control, but if team members feel that the objectives are not achievable, or the standards are too high, and believe that they are excluded from setting them, their level of commitment will not be very high and the overall performance of the team not as good as it could be. The manager may seem out of touch, the team can feel directionless and may even find itself torn by internal conflict and disagreement.

Many of the decisions about how to involve, who to involve and when are influenced by:

(a) the nature of the objectives and standards being set and their closeness to the overall objectives and core values of the organisation. Will they affect the whole organisation, a section, a group or team of individuals, or just one person?

(b) the degree of impact they will have on other people or the work of other parts of the organisation;

(c) the level of commitment required.

The C:E ratio was discussed above. You may also wish to consider how much certain individuals will be involved in achieving the objectives and whether they will be expected to demonstrate the desired standards in their behaviour (see Figure 2.2).

Figure 2.2: Contribution to the success of the objectives

High	Low	None
Those working closely to achieve the objectives. Those seen as role models or social leaders by the people required to meet the standards.	Those with a minor role in achieving the objectives. Those whose failure to meet the standards has low or little consequence.	Those to whom the objectives do not apply. Those not required to meet the standards or for whom the standards are not relevant.
Involve early in the process as they will need to own the objectives and demonstrate the standards on a regular basis.	Need to *understand* the objectives and what the standards mean in practice.	Need to be *aware* of the objectives in the context of the overall business and the relationship the standards have to those they are required to achieve.

You may also need to think about those people with a vested interest in the outcome of the objectives. Their actions or inactions, words and opinions will inevitably influence the success or failure of the objectives. Such people include the following.

1. **Those who directly control or can limit access to the resources you need.** These can be financial and physical resources and the goodwill of the people whose total commitment is essential. Early and full involvement of social leaders and influencers may be helpful.

2. **Those whose assistance will be needed.** This could be in the form of efforts, such as know-how or simply support. You may find you need the endorsement of a powerful person in the organisation to give you legitimacy and the authority to take the action needed.

3. **Those whose actions will be seen by others as demonstrations of the standards of performance will need to be highly committed to those standards.** We tend to forget how closely observed we are by our staff. Every minor action or behaviour pattern is seen and endowed with significance. Managers are role models and exemplars. If a new standard is being laid down for the staff, and key individuals are seen to ignore it, the chances of it being met will be very slim. We all know managers who have worked on the principle of 'do as I say, not as I do'.

The twin keys to unlock people's commitment are respect and honesty. If you expect people to be involved, demand their time and effort and ask their opinions, you have some obligation to take notice of what is said. If you totally ignore their views, the long-term effect could be worse than if you had not involved them at all. If you disagree or are unable to reflect their views, at the very least they deserve to know the reasons for your decision.

If you are not honest with people, you will find that your deception will be quickly known. People may not know whether or not you are keeping things from them or are telling the whole truth, but they will know that you are not being open with them.

They will try to guess at the truth of the matter and may be right. More often they will be wrong and may end up making decisions based on incorrect information. When they find out the truth, which usually happens in the long run, they could well lose their respect for you as their manager and as a person.

When to Involve People

The amount of time available often influences the level of involvement you believe to be possible. There may be times when circumstances will force your hand and you will need to make decisions alone or with just a few people. These decisions may be of major significance to your organisation and could well change its course and long-term objectives. Although you will need to obtain the commitment of everyone eventually, their early involvement may simply not be possible. Speed, confidentiality and closeness of fit with the organisation's underpinning values will be paramount. Nevertheless, you will need to take other action later to secure the staff's comprehension and active participation in the achievement of the objectives.

Often, however, we think there is less time than there actually is. We get pushed into making decisions too soon and alone when really we should take the time to think and involve other people. We are put under pressure to act and are not allowed the luxury of considering the effect the decisions will have on other people. But these other people may be the very ones who will be expected to put those decisions into action. Because we are being pressurised, we do not consider the consequences of their lack of agreement or commitment. If they had been involved they might have been able to point out the practical reasons why the objectives were unattainable and the standards impossible to meet.

Setting unrealisable standards and objectives can easily undermine your own position. Therefore a few moments' thought might pay dividends and save time later. Ask yourself whether it is quicker, in the long run, to take the time needed at the outset to involve the necessary people. If you do not involve them you may find that the time and energy you invest in setting the standards and objectives was wasted and other damage is done.

As well as deciding who, some thought should be given to the stages at which people should be involved and how much involvement is appropriate. It is possible to involve people during the following stages.

1. **The beginning.** Participation in the creation of the objectives and standards. For those objectives and standards whose attainment are important in the long-term but do not need immediate action. These often benefit from a broad discussion between all of those affected and the chance for reflection before deciding which course of action to take.

2. **The middle.** Negotiation about the meaning of the objectives and standards. For those which entail several options, the outcome of each would have different but equally 'good' results. Asking those involved for their opinions may help to resolve what could otherwise be a dilemma. When you are faced with an unclear situation, asking for views and suggestions from those not directly involved may help to clarify the problem and generate options previously not even thought about. It also secures their support as they may appreciate being asked for their opinions.

3. **Before the final setting.** Consultation with those directly affected. For those objectives and standards which are non-negotiable but require people to change their behaviour. People will need to understand what the changes will mean to them and what they will be expected to do in the future. They may need the opportunity to ask questions and time to talk and think about the implications before they fully comprehend what meeting the objectives and standards will involve. Giving them these opportunities will help achieve commitment rather than just compliance.

The following case shows how good intentions can lead to hell. The managing director had asked the office manager to provide a monthly report summarising the number of purchase orders raised in the previous period. So she decided to change the existing system which allowed the department managers to raise their own purchase orders up to the value of £1,000. The orders for amounts above this level were raised by the office manager and countersigned by the MD. The managers maintained files of their own orders and sent copies to the office manager.

The office manager decided that the easiest way of providing the MD's report would be for the department managers to make a monthly return of their orders to which she could simply add the larger amounts. Her staff, she decided, had too much to do to go through all the departments' copy orders and chase up any received by the end of the month.

Her decision caused uproar. She already had a poor working relationship with the department managers who saw her as bureaucratic and lacking in understanding of operational pressures. This latest measure confirmed the view that she was out of touch with reality. The managers reported their lack of confidence in her but explained that the problem was not simply due to this latest decision. Rather, it was the high-handed way she set standards that could not be attained and assumed they had nothing better to do with their time than carry out her administrative chores.

If she had asked them she would have discovered that they had been discussing the administrative systems and had some ideas which would simplify matters for them all, and improve the management information. This would have meant that everyone, including the MD, would have a better idea of how the money was flowing in and out of the business and how well it was performing overall.

Dealing with those who are Excluded

There may be times when it really is not possible to involve everyone in the establishment of the objectives and standards. We have already referred to those objectives and standards at the core of the organisation which must be met. Simply continuing to work for the organisation demonstrates commitment to these objectives and standards and the recognition of the need to comply with them.

There may be other times when you decide consciously that involvement is not:

1. **Appropriate.** When the objectives and standards are so close to the core of the organisation that only small number of key stakeholders can and should be involved. Wider participation would corrupt the process.

2. **Possible.** When time parameters, geographic location and nature of the task prevent the involvement of staff from taking place. However, you must make sure that the barriers are real; not just constructions erected by those who do not believe in a participative approach.

3. **Feasible.** When practical ways of making the involvement happen cannot be found. However, information technology and the increasing ease of email conferences is making open debate simpler and faster and is reducing the cost considerably.

4. **Desirable.** When the reasons for not involving staff outweigh the benefits in the short and long-term and are demonstrably so. You need to be clear what these reasons are and be aware of the counter arguments.

When you have decided who to include, you will have in effect decided who to exclude. You will then need to think about how to manage the people you have excluded in a positive way. To do this you will need to be clear about your reasons for not allowing them to participate in the processes. Sensitivity towards people who may be involved later in the achievement of the objectives is particularly important.

It is possible to make people feel part of the process without their having to contribute directly to it. This is achieved by telling them:

(a) what is happening;

(b) who is involved;

(c) why those people are involved (and others not);

(d) how the objectives and standards are being established;

(e) what progress is being made and the timescales involved;

(f) how the end results will be implemented and who will be involved.

We will return time and again to the importance of communication. As well as giving information, it is a recognition of people's interest in what is going on in their organisation and respects the part they play in the achievement of its objectives. Telling people what is happening in ways they are able to understand takes time and effort, so treating them as adults and keeping them informed has a cost. But treating them as if they are not interested will reduce the chance of them having any form of commitment to the organisation's objectives. Mushroom management (keeping people in the dark and giving them regular doses of manure) does not encourage people to make their best effort.

Open communication systems do not necessarily cost a lot of money. More often the cost is in terms of effort and is a matter of management style rather than the investment of large quantities of money. The greatest cost is likely to be time and this will be an opportunity cost. If you are not communicating with your staff what else are you doing with your time?

How to Involve

There are several techniques which you can use to improve the effectiveness of involving your staff. Asking people for their opinions in the corridor is a common approach but is not necessarily the most effective way of involving them formally in setting down the future direction of your organisation or section. Meetings are also common, but again, unless they are carefully structured, managed, and recorded, they can result in aimless discussions which go over the same ground time after time without reaching any resolution or agreement. The following may help you take a more participative approach which involves your staff and others in the establishment of objectives and standards.

Structured Meeting

The topic for discussion is broken down into an agenda comprised of small parts which are put together in a logical sequence that flows. Each item is dealt with fully, decisions are clearly expressed and agreement secured before the next topic is started. If there is any dissension, this is either recorded, deferred for future consideration or the discussion continued until the cause of the disagreement is resolved.

Such an agenda would include the questions below. The decisions taken would be recorded thus:

1. What is the desired outcome? What do we want to achieve?
   Increase our sales by 5 per cent.
2. What steps do we need to take to get there?
   Get more new customers and improve our after-sales service to get more repeat business.
3. What action is required to take those steps?
   Compete more fiercely in our existing markets and open up new markets by general advertising.

There are several ways to conduct such a meeting. Brain-storming is widespread but seldom used properly. The meeting's participants should be asked to contribute their ideas freely. These should be recorded on a flipchart or whiteboard. No questioning of their meaning or discussion of their value is allowed at this stage. Debate opens when all the ideas have been expressed and everyone has run out of ideas. Then clarification is gained, relative merits explored and decisions made about what to include and what to omit.

Surveys

It is possible to involve people and secure their views without holding a meeting. Surveys may be particularly appropriate if large numbers of people are to be involved, as their commitment to the results is essential for long-term success. Some companies make use of employee attitude surveys as a way of giving staff some means of influencing the organisation's behaviour.

Similar types of questionnaire can be used to gather views regarding the merits or demerits of certain courses of action (almost an in-house referendum). As with all such methods of canvassing opinion, the questions asked need to be very carefully thought out and the method for analysing the responses should be decided in advance. Closed questions (yes or no, or the use of tick boxes) make analysis easier but limit the chance of staff saying what they think. However, open questions are difficult to analyse.

You should also think beforehand about how you will treat the results. If you are not prepared to go public about the outcome, especially if you think you may not agree with it, do not ask the questions. A lack of response can be more demoralising than not asking.

Another way of structuring the questionnaire is to use paired comparisons. This technique is used in market research to find out what people think about a number of related topics. Each of the topics is matched in turn against another and respondents are asked to give each a rating. This is done until every topic is compared to all the others.

For example, an organisation decides to ask its staff which pattern of behaviour, in their view, draws the best reaction from its customers so that its initial training can be better targeted. They are asked to rate the following out of a possible eleven points.

- Greet all customers with a smile.
- Use the customer's name.

- Use the customer's name.
- Shake hands on greeting.

- Deal with only one person at once.
- Shake hands on greeting.

- Use the customer's name.

- Greet all customers with a smile.
- Answer all telephone calls within five rings.
- Deal with only one person at once.

This approach will enable you to canvas the opinions of large numbers of people (or a representative sample) and determine the comparative importance for each standard of behaviour in relation to the others.

2.7 SUMMARY

This chapter has described what organisational objectives and standards of performance are like and has looked at how they can be established in ways that allow members of the organisation to contribute to the process. We have considered the effects of not involving people appropriately and explored how they may be included in ways that result in a high level of commitment to their achievement.

The next chapter will move on to discuss how those objectives and standards can be used to guide action and inform the monitoring of performance. It will also look at how appraisal of objective criteria can be used to support learning.

3

HOW TO MONITOR AND APPRAISE PERFORMANCE

3.1 INTRODUCTION

Having spent time and energy establishing your organisation's objectives and standards, no doubt you will be interested to know whether they are being attained and maintained. Progress towards the achievement of your targets will need to be watched and you will want to make sure that levels of performance do not slip. This is done through monitoring and appraisal systems. This chapter will look at what needs to be done to control operations in ways that ensure the effort and energy of your staff are being channelled in the right directions. It will also tell you how and what to measure and what to do about those aspects of performance that cannot be measured.

You can use the results of the monitoring and appraisal in positive ways. The feedback can be shared, reflected upon, and the experiences can be instructive. Alternatively, the results can be used as a weapon, to allocate blame. Drawing attention to failure can produce sticks with which to beat the people concerned. This approach does not encourage people to work to their best effect. It frightens them and creates an atmosphere in which protecting one's own back comes before achieving the organisation's objectives. If you want people to work well and make the best use of their abilities, you need to find ways of enabling them to do so. The information generated through monitoring can be used constructively to create this sort of climate and provide a means of enhancing capabilities. The monitoring can also be used in support of planning and to prevent things from going wrong.

Nevertheless, things do go wrong. We will look at some of the reasons behind failures and discuss how good quality feedback systems will help you spot the first signs of things not going quite as you intend. We will then look at some types of remedial action that can be taken to prevent small mistakes from developing into full-scale disasters. Finally, we will look at how you can build on the results of your experience and learning to stop some of the more common errors happening in the first place.

3.2   WHAT TO CONTROL

There is little point in trying to control the uncontrollable or those things that do not matter, but when organisations, especially those that have existed for a long time, are closely scrutinised, there is a high chance that you will find elaborate and costly systems that do just that. Financial matters are particularly prone to this practice.

One publicly funded organisation, with the obvious need to ensure that its funds were properly used and fully accounted, had a detailed checking system in place to ensure that its staff did not fiddle their travel expense claims. Most of the staff were based in district offices and had to drive considerable distances to do their jobs. Each month they were required to give their manager a completed and detailed sheet showing the miles travelled and the expenses being claimed. The manager was expected to check and sign off each form. The forms were sent to the finance department where again they were checked before being passed for payment. Any inaccurate forms were returned to the manager so that the member of staff could be confronted with their mistake. The organisation, under pressure to cut costs, decided to find out how many fraudulent claims were being made and how much the procedure saved.

The finance director was somewhat shocked to find that the only thing being checked was the staff's ability to add up and multiply. No one was checking to see if the journeys were needed or whether they were being made at all. Just checking on basic mathematical skills was taking a lot of staff and managerial time with no cost-effective outcome. In fact the opposite was true.

Often simple mistakes were blown out of proportion, generating unnecessary disputes between finance staff, managers and staff.

The matters that should be controlled are those directly relating to the organisation's core business and its values – those are the things that matter and are likely to have major consequences for the organisation. Too often you may get excited about things that seem really important at the time, but after a week, you wonder what all the fuss was all about. If you are to put energy into creating control mechanisms and re-focus resources from the core business onto internal systems and procedures, you need to be sure that they will add value to the organisation; that they are not just a drain.

Well-written objectives include indicators to help to assess progress towards their achievement. They will also have milestones or targets that show whether or not the objective is being achieved. These are intended to keep everyone on course and give priority to those actions related to the objectives. It is surprisingly easy to get pulled off course. A good objective statement looks like that outlined in Figure 3.1.

Figure 3.1: Objective statement

Objective: to increase customer spending

Target A
- Improve customer satisfaction.

Action Step 1
- Enhance staff's customer relations skills through intensive, targeted training.

Indicator of Progress 1
- 75 per cent of staff completing the course successfully within six months. The remainder to be in progress.

The aim is to ensure 100 per cent successful completion within twelve months.

Control Systems

The control systems for the above example would ensure that:

(a) staff in the priority group attended the required training;

(b) the participants were passing the course at the required rate;

(c) plans were in place for other staff to attend;

(d) remedial action was being taken to help those not passing the course to do so within the required timescale;

(e) staff were putting into practice their learning during their transactions with customers;

(f) customer satisfaction was increasing;

(g) customers were spending more money.

Control mechanisms should draw attention to the organisation's values and basic standards. These should reflect the organisation's core business and underpinning ethos. So, for example, if one manager was not sending staff on the training course because a new computer system was being installed, it is easier to deal with the conflicting priorities.

The work of American psychologist, B F Skinner, contains some interesting ideas for managers. Although his research is regarded by some as simplistic as most of it was done with animals, there are some notions that can be used to help understand people. He argued that people, like animals, respond to stimuli. Even though people have choices over their behaviour and can control their actions, they tend to behave without thought. They react rather than give a considered response. Therefore, if a pattern of behaviour is rewarded consistently, an individual will learn that by performing those actions a reward will follow. They learn that events have a cause and a reaction; they also learn the connection between other actions and punishment. In this way, patterns of behaviour are reinforced and become part of the individual's normal repertoire. This thinking, with other theories of motivation, underpins such schemes as performance-related pay.

People, however, are more complex than this. Unless there is a clear link between desired behaviours and the available rewards or punishments, unintended consequences can occur. Most parents know that giving sweets to stop a young child from screaming can result in that child learning that screaming is the way to get sweets. The same thing can happen at work. Take, for example, the case of a famous wire company which established production targets for its managers, including increased output and better productivity. One manager, in charge of wire fencing production, decided to be clever and produce as much of the easiest type of fencing as possible. Instead of going for chicken wire, the highest selling product but the slowest to produce, he decided to go for large quantities of large gauge fencing – the sort used to secure cows and horses. This needed strong, high quality wire so it was comparatively expensive to make, but because the holes were big, production was fast. What the manager did not consider was how much of this type of wire was sold each year compared to chicken wire. He exceeded his production targets wonderfully but the company was stuck with a five-year stock of an expensive product.

Control systems should focus on those aspects of the company's operations that cannot be compromised. Examples include:

(a) safety;

(b) customer treatment;

(c) financial propriety;

(d) honesty;

(e) compliance with the law;

(f) ethics and organisational values;

(g) achievement of key objectives.

In the case of the latter, it is also important to establish systems that give clarity to the means as well as the ends. Otherwise, you may find yourself with large quantities of unsaleable cow wire, instead of profitable chicken wire.

The use of physical resources should also be controlled in appropriate ways. As a manager, regardless of your level in the organisation's hierarchy, every day you are using up other people's possessions, property and money. You need to be aware of this responsibility and be prepared to be accountable to your employer for the proper use of their resources. Hopefully the days of having to hand in the pencil stub before being issued with a new one have long gone. If people are trusted they usually respond accordingly. Similarly, if they know they are not being trusted, their behaviour will reflect this lack of faith. If you treat adults like children, they will behave like children.

The publicly funded organisation referred to in the first example above decided to replace control with trust. Its aim was to foster a culture built on partnership and delegate responsibility and decision making to a point closest to its clients. Managers were encouraged to be open with their staff, and staff were asked to participate more in decisions that affected them and their services. The intention was for them to be more involved and feel a greater sense of responsibility for their actions. The finance director decided to take a risk. Each member of staff who used their car frequently was given a budget for mileage. Each budget was based on the amount claimed on average over the previous period. The individual was asked to sign for their own budget and it was made clear that there would be no additional funds unless the individual's duties changed substantially. Management time was saved and staff, it was found, repaid the trust placed in them by economising on their travel and reducing what were, presumably, unnecessary journeys. Nearly all budgets were underspent at the end of the financial year.

3.3   WHAT NOT TO CONTROL

Some organisations appear to believe they own their employees and have the right, through the contract of employment, to control what the staff think. This is a mistaken belief and can lead an employer into all kinds of difficulty. Even the most totalitarian of states has not been able to control the thoughts of its citizens. If an employer tries to enforce such degree of control, it will find itself alienating the people whose support and involvement it requires to succeed. While a state can ultimately dictate and police through rules and fear, an organisation cannot. It requires willing participation for its staff have a choice: they can leave.

Instead of trying to control the uncontrollable, it is far easier to accept that each individual has every right to hold their own beliefs and opinions and that this right is beyond the employment contract. An employer's rights extend only to those items specified in the explicit and implicit terms of that contract. These concern what an individual does within the scope of their role within the organisation and their responsibilities. Their personal values are no concern of the employer as long as they do not affect the individual's standard of work, the organisation and other members or erupt into open conflict. When they do start to affect any of these, the individual and employer will have to come to some understanding. If a compromise is not possible, the only course of action that may remain is a parting. We will consider later how the ending of the employment relationship can be handled in a positive way.

Similarly, what an individual does in their own free time is their own concern. However, there are occasions when these activities affect their employment and an employer feels there is a legitimate need to have some form of control over what an individual does outside their working hours. Any potential conflict of interests needs to be discussed openly. An easy example is the employee, perhaps a research scientist with irreplaceable specialist knowledge, who is working on a major project on the brink of breakthrough and is known to have a love of bungy jumping. Does the employer have the right to ask the scientist to put the weekend sport on hold until the completion of the project?

Other areas of an individual's private life may or may not have an impact on the employing organisation. These tend to fall into two categories:

(a) activities that bring an individual into the public eye;

(b) activities that may lead to a breach of the law.

The first category could include activities such as public office, voluntary or charity work or involvement in sporting or other competitive events. The employer could support these kinds of pastime to demonstrate the organisation's commitment to community activities. The individual's success will be seen as reflected glory on the organisation and its social responsibility. On the other hand, would an employee's acclaimed lead in the local amateur dramatic society's raucous production of *The Rockie Horror Show* be seen as contributing to the reputation of the company?

The second category can lead you, the manager, and the employing organisation to deep questioning of your core values.

1. What would you do if a well-regarded member of your staff was photographed during a raid on the premises of a suspected peddler of pornography and the picture was published on the front page of the local newspaper?

2. Would you keep an individual on your employee list while they served a prison sentence for a driving offence when their job does not involve driving?

3. How would you deal with someone fined for possessing cannabis?

These examples ask you to consider how far an individual's private life affects their ability to perform their job to the standard you require. What right does an employer have to control employees' private lives and how far does that right extend?

We highlighted above the need to focus on what *really* matters: those aspects of performance, actions or inactions that contribute to the achievement of the organisation's or the section's objectives and standards. As a manager you should be sure you can answer the questions below.

1. How do you know if all your staff, systems and operations are doing what they should be doing? What would happen if they were not?

2. When you come back from holiday, how do you know that satisfactory progress is being made?

3. What do you do with the management information you generate or receive?

4. Does it help you answer the above questions? Do you work on it or does it simply fill the waste bin?

5. If it does not, where and how do you get the information you need?

3.4   WHAT AND HOW TO MEASURE

We have agreed that trying to control the unimportant is a waste of energy, time and resources. Trying to measure the immeasurable is equally a futile exercise. Yet many organisations attempt to do just that. We often discuss the need for quality and the importance in maintaining and improving it but when asked to define what we mean we struggle. We devise elaborate control mechanisms but find it difficult to demonstrate improvement year on year or prove that the actions we have taken have had any effect.

We confuse the tangible and intangible and seek to find direct links between cause and effect. We also get trapped in the fiction that measurement is an essential part of modern management. This thinking implies that all important aspects of running a successful organisation can be counted and only those aspects that can be countered are important. One reason for the popularity of this approach is that it is comparatively easy to focus on the countable. Also, it must be said that many organisations operate very well, relying on these measures to tell them how well they are doing.

Measures of the tangible are valuable for they can draw attention to key aspects of performance and can be used as indicators. They can be drawn from the objectives, as we saw above, and used to assess whether the actions taken are approaching the targets at which they are aimed. It is not unknown for people to work extremely hard and be very successful while doing the wrong things.

Take the case of the sales team who decided to create a new set of promotional material for one of their company's products. They spent a long time creating a number of different themes and approaches. They designed several new publicity leaflets and obtained quotations from printers and distribution agencies. They considered the comparative values of bus and roadside posters and obtained a number of quotations. They were pleased and excited about the results of their labours and booked time with the marketing manager to present their work.

The appointed time came and the team made their presentation. They were pleased with their performance but were a little puzzled by the marketing manager's lack of enthusiasm.

"Well done, everyone," he said. "You have done a fine piece of work. I like your ideas and am impressed by the amount of research and background work you have done. It is a shame that we are withdrawing this particular product next year. Didn't you read the marketing plan before you started?"

Most often measures focus attention on the way resources are being used. They might include the following.

Money

Most managers are used to working to revenue budgets. These are the amounts of money allocated each year and may or may not be related to levels of activity. They can be presented in terms of how much expenditure is expected or used to show the flow of funds in and out. The level of sophistication will reflect the nature of your business, the amount of responsibility you have and the culture of your organisation. Used intelligently, a budget can be a management tool which helps you to run your business tightly and efficiently. It can indicate where slack resources are being hidden and highlight possible areas where cash may be leaking from the business. Used badly, however, it becomes a weapon to beat managers and staff. A typical example is the use of poor trading figures to berate employees who have no influence on the level of business.

Few managers have control over capital funds, or believe they do not control them. Capital funds are the financial resources used for long-term investments and are usually shown separately on company balance sheets. Operational funds, revenue budgets and trading figures are in one set of accounts and investments in another. For the most part, the managers involved in long-term operations have access to such capital monies.

The measures show if the expenditure is in accordance with the forecast and indicates any deviation from estimates monitored. Most often concern is focused on overspend and underspends are seen as bonuses. This may be mistaken celebration. Using the measures as indicators of what is happening may reveal that the underspends are a result of reducing quality or shortcutting. These may, in the long run, prove to be expensive economies.

Monetary indicators need to be used wisely. This means reading the data accurately and using it as an indicator, a prompt to ask questions about what is happening. You should remember that the flow of money shows only part of the overall picture. Budget figures should always be used alongside other data. Information thus produced is used to reflect fully, and in its entirety, on the state of the operation or organisation.

Inputs

Inputs are easily counted as often they are bought in from other suppliers. Examples of inputs purchased or obtained for a price by an organisation include:

(a) raw materials for processing in the creation of goods and services;

(b) supplies used in administration of the organisation;

(c) the costs of the premises required to house staff and carry out the business;

(d) the running costs of those premises.

Other inputs include the hidden costs of running the business, such as accountancy and legal fees, insurance and advisory services.

The other major input into any organisation comes from the staff employed to produce the goods and services and to run the organisation. Counting the hours worked is easy when there is a direct relationship between the time spent on an operation and the value of the outcome. For example, in catering, a rule of thumb is used to calculate the rough selling price of a dish. The cost of raw goods represents one-third of the selling price, labour costs another third and overheads and profit the remaining third. The same sort of rough calculation can be made for professional workers, such as solicitors, whose time is spent on one case. Their input hours can be recorded and charged accordingly. It is less easy to attribute and count the hours of input into areas of work where results do not necessarily reflect the amount of time spent doing the job. Knowledge management is an emerging issue for the 21st century.

An example of this can be found in creative occupations. A designer, for example, may be inspired today and be able to produce a high-quality piece of work in a comparatively short period of time. Tomorrow, however, a job of far inferior quality may take twice as long. Using hours of work as a measure would be inappropriate in this case.

Outputs

The results of the inputs, i.e. the outputs, are also often counted. For example, the number of goods produced and sold, customers served, contracts agreed can be recorded and measured to demonstrate effectiveness, or productivity. Other outputs, by-products and wastage, can also be counted. These are useful both to measure the efficiency of the people involved in the process and the process itself. Sometimes, however, it is not always possible to discern which is which.

A production line was known not to be working as well as it might. It was running at only 60 per cent efficiency and producing many faulty goods. When asked about what was going wrong, the staff on the line said that the maintenance routines were being cut short and the line was breaking down too often, resulting in a lot of down time and damage to the goods in progress. The maintenance staff said that the routines were being followed correctly, but the staff on the line were messing about and not paying attention to what they were doing. This meant that operating routines were not being followed correctly and the simple remedial steps needed to correct any small deviations were not being taken. These led to breakdowns and stoppages.

The numbers will tell you that productivity is down and may draw your attention to problem areas, but they will not help you diagnose the cause.

Stocks

Inventory control can provide many hours of fun. Counting stock and work in progress and checking them against goods-received notices, invoices, job sheets, customer orders and sales, can keep staff occupied for days, if not weeks. Auditing is important, please do not underestimate its value. It is the only sure way to prove any misdoings or acts of fraud. And we do know that some people steal goods and materials from their employers.

In deciding the type of stock control systems you need to put in place, and planning how you are going to run them, you should consider the balance between the risk and possible cost of loss, against the cost and effect of running the system. Questions you may wish to ask can include the following:

1. What is the chance of stock going missing as a result of:

    (a) carelessness;

    (b) wastage and misuse;

    (c) theft or fraud?

2. How elaborate a control system do you want to set up?

3. How much are you prepared to pay to run the system?

4. How does this compare with the likely cost of lost goods and materials?

5. When do you want to control stock:

    (a) at the point of entry;

    (b) in store;

    (c) at the point of use;

    (d) at a point in time (e.g. six monthly or annually)?

6. What message will you give your staff if the control system implies to them that you do not trust them?

7. Will the benefits accrued by your chosen stock control system outweigh the full cost of running it?

Customers

Knowing who your customers are and who is using your services are vital pieces of information. You will need them for your business and development plans and for the effective marketing of your products and services. If you do not have this knowledge, you will be pitching in the dark.

Yet many organisations do just that. The information, in general, held about customers, their habits and preferences, is of a woefully poor quality. The National Vocational Qualification Standards in Customer Service have attempted to improve on this situation. They include, as units and elements, indicators of good practice. Although the real reason for the production of these Standards was to recognise the skills of staff and identify areas where their abilities could be developed, they can also be used to suggest areas where you could improve your organisation's practices.

For example, the need for keeping records is included in the Standard. As a minimum you need to know who is buying your goods or using your services. This will probably be in the form of a customer profile. You should also know who has stopped doing business with you and why. Knowledge of your market segment, potential customers and their requirements will help develop your business by indicating where you should target your activities to attract new customers. A great deal of marketing effort is wasted by generalised or inappropriate targeting. Poor performance is not just a waste of resources. Even the most dedicated individual, who puts their effort and hopes into developing their customer base but encounter repeated failure, will eventually lose their enthusiasm.

If pay and performance assessments are based on customer activity levels and growth, it is essential that staff have the information they need to monitor the behaviour of their customers and target their efforts in the most effective directions. It is also reasonable for them to expect that their performance will be assessed on good quality information. This should be gathered over the whole period under review and be based on accurate and unambiguous data.

Staff

You need to have some basic factual information about the people who work for you. Considering how long you spend with others at work you probably know surprisingly little about each other. This is not just personal information, but the sort of information you need in order to manage your workforce, deploy people to their best effect, develop their skills and plan for their future and yours.

Certain information is needed for legal purposes and is required to help you put together statutory and financial returns. This includes, for example, the number of people who work in your organisation, the hours they work, the amount they are paid and other emoluments and benefits they might receive. Other data is demographic, for example, age and length of service. You also need to know about turnover and reasons why individuals have left your employment. This information will draw attention to possible problems. For example, high turnover can be indicative of poor management or team relationship difficulties, lack of training, mismatched expectations or poaching by a competitor. It also informs plans for succession by helping you predict future staffing requirements and anticipate forthcoming events.

The most obvious of these is retirement. Some people maintain that succession planning and the implementation of an equal opportunities policy are contradictory and that one negates the other. This is not so. Succession planning means looking at future requirements and preparing all those with the potential to meet those needs. Many of the so-called fast track management development programmes operate on this basis. They work in the following way.

1. A company estimates that its annual turnover amongst managers will be X per cent. This is done by calculating the number of leavers as a percentage of the total number of staff employed in that category during the year.

2. It recruits that number of trainee managers, often graduates, including the allowance for their turnover.

3. These individuals are trained and their skills developed.

4. As their development programme lasts a number of years, the contents are adapted to take account of changes in the company's business and its skill needs.

5. The trainees are appointed to substantive management posts as vacancies arise and are promoted to the level of their abilities.

6. Any shortfall of managers is filled by other internal and possibly external recruitment.

This process complements the equality of opportunity, as it is based on an explicit process and the route is transparent. Initial recruitment is open and is based on clearly specified criteria. All trainees can see what they need to do to progress. Promotion is based on the assessment of ability and suitability rather than as a result of a competitive process.

In addition to turnover and the basic facts about your employees, you will find that, to manage your people effectively, you will need other measures. For example, you will need to know about your staff's attendance patterns and sickness levels. Some organisations, particularly smaller ones, believe they know their staff well enough to do without formal records. Most often, this is true and problems do not occur, but when they do, you will find that they will have crept up on you before you realised it. Then you are faced with a difficult situation without any information on which to base and justify your decisions.

Take the case of James, a middle-aged salesman in a company of 25 staff. No records had been kept as the MD knew each person well. The newest member of staff had been there for nearly two years and James had been employed for the last fifteen. The MD began to notice that James was not looking very well, but put it down to the after effects of the flu most people had suffered. His sales were a bit down, but the MD was sure they would pick up again once he got over it.

The other sales staff began individually to notice that things were not right with James. He missed a monthly team meeting and was not seen in the office as often as before. One of his customers made a comment about him appearing not to be as smart as normal and asked after his health. Another rang to find out why he had missed an appointment. Each of these incidents seemed inconsequential in themselves but together they were indicators of a developing problem.

After several months of minor incidents, James arrived at work one day asking to see the MD urgently. He had just received a twelve-month driving ban for drink driving. It turned out that he had a drink problem that had been gradually worsening. When asked why he hadn't told the MD about it before James said he had been ashamed of himself and had hoped that someone would notice that he had been making mistakes. When he was alone again, the MD reflected on recent events and realised all the signs had been there but no one had put the pieces of the jigsaw together. He was relieved, however, that nothing more dreadful had happened to James.

If you keep good quality information about staff you will find that using it intelligently will help you to identify these and similar problems in their early stages. Records should not be kept for their own sake or to police or control staff, their role is to monitor progress and performance against shared standards. If they do not do this they are not effective and should be scrapped in favour of a more useful system.

3.5   THINGS YOU CANNOT MEASURE

Some standards can not be assessed by the measurement of numeric factors. These generally concern the quality rather than the quantity of performance. Increasingly organisations are finding that quality makes the difference. As business moves more towards the provision of services rather than the production of goods, achieving intangible objectives give one organisation the competitive edge over another. Assessment of quality is potentially fraught with problems and can leave a manager open to accusations of dealing in fuzzy wuzzies, favouritism or even discrimination. This is particularly so if judgements about people's pay, prospects and promotion depend on such decisions being made on intangible criteria.

If you have no fixed point against which to make such assessments, maintaining consistency over time and between different individuals becomes difficult, if not impossible. Your views are influenced by recent events and occasionally by factors that have nothing to do with the situation or person under assessment. You may also change your mind over time. Something that was of vital importance a year ago may seem trivial now. If you want to be seen as a good manager, the demonstration of your abilities to treat all members of your staff fairly and consistently over time will be essential.

This does not mean that you should treat everybody in exactly the same way all of the time. Obviously, you need to be flexible and take account of the needs and differences of each individual. However, you do need to ensure that differences in treatment are really needed and that everyone is managed in the same, consistent fashion. How do you achieve such a state? How can intangible standards and qualitative aspects of performance be assessed against measures?

First, you need to be clear about what is meant by fair and consistent treatment. Using the process recommended in Chapter 2 works equally well for this purpose.

Second, you need to know what behaviour falls below the standard required and what exceeds that expected. As well as asking what is fair and consistent, ask yourself (and your staff) what is not fair and inconsistent. The answers will give you statements of high quality performance which can be compared to poor performance. For example, see Figure 3.2.

Figure 3.2: Comparison of fair and unfair behaviour

Fair	Unfair
Uses criteria which are known to everyone and understood.	Uses private and personal opinions.
Gathers information over the whole of the review period.	Uses the last example as typical evidence.
Uses a number of sources for the information on which judgements are made.	Listens only to the views of the favourite few.
Seeks for information from all those with a valid contribution and weighs differing opinions to arrive at a considered decision.	Seeks information that confirms first decision and rejects any that discounts it.
Is prepared to amend views if new information becomes available.	Sticks rigidly to first decision.

Making the criteria explicit changes them from being intangible to tangible, capable of being discussed, debated and assessed. It does not mean that their qualitative nature is removed and that they are changed into yet more aspects of performance to be counted, they become instead statements of behaviour, either that required or not. The statements can be assessed, not counted, and the subjective element of the judgement be reduced. It is not possible to make the judgement of one human being by another totally objective; we all bring our own prejudices and perceptions to bear on the process. But it is possible to take account of this and introduce means of moderating it. For example, it is possible to create rating scales to ascertain how well the quality standard is being achieved.

If we take one of the above statements as an example we can show how this can be done by allocating points to the description of fair behaviour.

- 4 points = seeks information from all those with a valid contribution and weighs differing opinions to arrive at a considered decision.

- 1 point = seeks information that confirms first decision and rejects any that discounts it.

- 2 points = seeks information and listens to other points of view, but rejects them.

- 3 points = seeks information and accepts differing points of view but does not consider them when making the decision.

This gives a four-point ranking scale against which the standard of performance can be assessed. The scale if used over time gives a consistency and also means that other people can assess the performance of an individual and come up with the same result.

Results

You should not talk immediately to the people whose performance you have measured. Instead, you should think about what you are going to say and how you are going to say it. Feedback is essential to help the people concerned maintain their standards, improve on them and learn how to do things better. However, if the messages are badly constructed and the process is handled in a clumsy fashion, the receiver is unlikely to act on the information. We will discuss below how to give good quality feedback. Only when you have given some thought to the matter should you talk to the people concerned.

Even when the results are not good, the individual or individuals concerned need to know, if they are going to do something about their performance. If the provision of the feedback is handled well, they will be better able to reflect on the reasons for the results. They will be more inclined to consider possible areas of substandard performance and identify what remedial measures need to be taken to correct failures and improve on weaknesses. At the very least they deserve the chance to improve. If you feel that the results are so bad that they should not have this chance, you should ask what has happened to make the performance levels fall off. If you and your staff have been open with each other over time, surprises of this nature should not arise.

If performance has deteriorated very rapidly, you need to ask many other questions so that the real reasons (not just symptoms) can be identified. Returning to the case of James, the salesman, the warning signs were there if only the manager had been aware of them and had used good quality information as the basis for regular review of performance.

If the level of achievement exceeds that expected, the results of the review can be publicised and success celebrated. Good performance deserves genuine praise and acknowledgement. It provides examples to demonstrate to others what is expected and the recognition encourages them to raise their standards. Some organisations use internal competition for this very reason. Rewards provided range from 'employee of the month' awards to payments in the form of commission or bonuses. Some companies, especially in highly competitive industries, invest heavily in incentive schemes as a way of encouraging people to try harder and achieve higher standards of performance. 'Points equal prizes' schemes, which extend to holidays, cars and other high value goods, are believed to be motivators leading to excellence.

Some organisations are sceptical about the use of such mechanisms and do not believe that they lead to improved levels of performance which endure. Some managers believe that they can actually damage organisational cohesiveness by fostering internal competition which can turn in on itself and the wish to win can detract from collaboration. The focus shifts from the long-term, overall objectives to short-term, individual success.

This is not to say that a manager should not draw attention to good performance and reward the individual. The reward, however should be appropriate. This means fitting the organisation's culture, the scale of the success, the degree of effort made by those concerned in achieving and the value of the achievement to all concerned. It should also be in a form of 'currency' that is of value to the individual.

Moreover, achievement can be used as an opportunity for learning. We all know the expression 'we learn from our mistakes', but while, sometimes, mistakes might create opportunities for licking our wounds rather than reflecting on the experience, we all tend to accept that the weaker aspects of our performance can be improved. Failures are events not to be repeated and areas where skills and knowledge are known to be lacking need to be remedied. But how often do we consciously analyse success to identify:

(a) the aspects of performance that led to the achievement;

(b) the strengths that need to be maintained;

(c) the skills and areas of knowledge which need to be developed by others to make the standard of achievement widespread?

3.6 FEEDBACK

Giving bad news is not easy, but sometimes, giving good news is even worse. Some people find praising other people highly embarrassing. It need not be so, if some very simple rules are followed. These can work too when feeding back information about those areas of work in need of improvement and those which have resulted in higher than expected levels of achievement.

Ten Rules for Giving Feedback

1. Feedback should be of value to the receiver rather than be given to satisfy the motives of the provider.
2. Timing and location should be considered.
3. The feedback should be related to specific examples of behaviour rather than general or abstract comments.
4. Ideas and information should be shared rather than the receiver be told what they should or should not do.
5. Alternatives should be explored rather than answers and solutions provided.
6. The emphasis should be on *what* is said rather than *why* it is said.
7. The focus should be on:
   (a) behaviour rather than the person;
   (b) the essential aspects of performance which the receiver can use rather than giving large quantities of information;
   (c) observation of what actually happened rather than inferences from what might have occurred or assumptions about motives;
   (d) description of the performance rather than judgement on the outcomes.
8. Checks should be made to ensure that the communication has been understood and the feedback received accurately.
9. The receiver can refuse to accept the feedback.

10. The reasons for giving the feedback should be explicit – if it is not intended to help the individual do better next time, do not give it.

3.7 WHY THINGS GO WRONG

With the best will in the world, not even the brightest employee can get everything right all of the time. Sometimes, as in the case of James, things begin to slip or go wrong. The reason for measuring is to help you step in early and stop performance falling below an acceptable standard. This can help you prevent it adversely affecting the quality of production, levels of service or the achievement of objectives.

Before you rush in to take such action, however, spend a few moments thinking why performance standards might be falling. These thoughts will help you prepare yourself. Do not try to answer for the individual or to guess what is happening or anticipate the reasons. The only way to find out the truth of the situation is by hearing what the person concerned has to say. Your thoughts should be to prepare your questions and gather together the information you already have about the person.

Insight and understanding will enable you to comprehend why:

(a) people fail to achieve, even when they know what is expected;

(a) they say that they understand what is expected even when events clearly show they do not;

(b) they fail to meet standards they were previously able to exceed easily.

Human Error

People sometimes get things wrong. They misread situations, misunderstand what is said to them or get locked into the wrong line of thought. The human brain makes errors. Most of us can remember, possibly with some embarrassment, times when we have done 'stupid' things like putting the coffee jar in the fridge and the milk in the cupboard, calling someone we know very well by the wrong name or driving on automatic pilot back to our old home six months after moving house. Most of the time, simple errors in thought patterns, such as these, have no lasting consequences, at other times they can be catastrophic. These kinds of mistake occur when the individual's mind is busy with other things. The causes of preoccupation can include the following.

Stress

Too much to think about. In other words there are too many thoughts in the individual's mind. Too many demands are being made of the individual. The person cannot work out which thing to do or which problem to solve first. The pressure to perform is more than the individual can respond to, leading to a form of paralysis. This can be called the 'headless chicken' syndrome.

Different Priorities

The individual can not distinguish between the urgent and the important. Possibly, events and the words and actions of others have clouded the objectives. Conflicting demands from other people can also make it impossible to decide what to do first.

Lack of Concentration

The individual, for whatever reason, may simply have allowed their mind to wander. This can be due to other factors, such as stress and tiredness rather than a lack of self-discipline.

Tiredness

The individual may be tired. They could have had too many late nights, enjoying themselves, or they may be approaching exhaustion caused by overwork. The problem of the long hours culture is slowly being recognised but many still fight to be the first at work in the morning and the last away at night, armed with a bulging bag of homework. They allow themselves no breaks during the day and work all weekend. This type of excessiveness takes its toll over time. The addiction to work becomes obsessive and the individual forgets how to relax.

Exhaustion does not happen immediately. It builds up gradually. During this time mistakes are made, judgement becomes impaired and things are forgotten. Doing something else even for a short time refreshes the brain and leads to improved performance. Recreation is also re-creation.

Boredom

People get fed up and bored by doing the same thing repeatedly. This is normal. Many need new challenges and ideas to keep them fresh and interested. However, essentially, for most people, the brain is lazy. It does not willingly seek work, but purposeful mental exercise is essential if the mind is to be kept healthy and alert. Without mental effort and fitness, people stop thinking about what they are doing and let their minds go on automatic pilot, just ticking along. They do not pay attention and mistakes happen.

Sabotage

People sometimes make mistakes deliberately. Industrial sabotage can take two forms: pure malevolence when the individual sets out to do damage for evil reasons and vengeance. The motives behind malevolent actions vary but the effect is the same. Something is spoilt – often for other people. Vengeance arises when the individual, for some reason, feels aggrieved and wants to make other people pay for causing them pain. In organisational life, the others are often *them*: the bosses or you, the manager.

Inadequate Skills or Knowledge

Some mistakes happen because people do not have the skills or knowledge needed so they are unable to perform to the standard required. It is not unusual for people to say they have the skills needed until experience proves otherwise. It is possible that they have lied and deliberately misled you. It is also possible that the individual has overrated their own abilities. People often believe they are better than they really are and events can provide a painful lesson.

Incompetence

Some mistakes are caused when people try to do a task that is beyond them. They may try because they have overestimated their abilities, or they could have started the task because they have been pressurised into doing the job. The reasons will vary but the results will be the same. They will fail to achieve the objectives or meet the standard because of a lack of skill or knowledge.

Incapability

Incapability is different from incompetence. Although the result is the same – the job not being doing properly – the cause is different. The failure to perform may be caused by physical or mental health problems, a disability or circumstances. The problem may be permanent or temporary. Depending on the individual, their previous contribution and the reason for their incapability, you may decide to be tolerant. Adjustments can be made to accommodate the individual's particular needs. These can be very practical and simple measures. Often all the person requires is the support and time needed to return to their previous level of ability.

In many countries individuals with a chronic or enduring disability are protected by the equivalent of the UK's Disability Discrimination Act. Employers are responsible for making reasonable adjustments to help such people do their job, within the scope of their abilities. Advice is available from the government and many support agencies.

There will be times, however, when it is not possible to accommodate the individual. The genuine needs of the business prevent allowances and adjustments being made. If you are certain nothing reasonably can be done to help and there is no other part of the organisation where the individual can be deployed, it is possible to terminate their contract of employment. Under the terms of the UK's employment legislation, a dismissal as a result of the individual's incapability (providing proper procedures have been followed) would not be wrongful.

Poor Attitude

An individual, whose attitude is not up to standard, can also be responsible for mistakes. You can excuse some mistakes caused by stress or excessive tiredness. Mistakes made as a result of carelessness, lack of attention, negligence or sloppy work cannot be justified in the same way. As a manager, you will be required to take action to deal with such attitudes. However, before you check your rights and responsibilities under the terms of the employment legislation, spend a few moments considering why the individual's attitude has changed. This will be useful and may, in the long-term, prevent you going down the wrong road. (This, of course, assumes that you did not make a poor selection decision in the first place.)

It could be that you have failed to detect a developing problem, as in the case of James. Before taking the final step of dismissing the individual, you might be able to recover the situation by taking appropriate disciplinary and remedial action.

Systems Failure

Systems are necessary for the smooth running of any form of enterprise. Even self-employed writers need to keep records and have internal administrative systems.

Unfotunately administrative systems tend to transmute and acquire a life form of their own. They develop, grow and evolve.

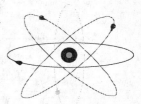

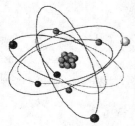

From a simple form they multiply and expand, taking on a far more complex, multi-faceted shape. Eventually they become so entangled it is not possible to distinguish one system from another.

Any system is prone to failure. Parts simply stop working. Sometimes they wear out or become outmoded; sometimes they just break down from over or incorrect use.

As systems become more complex, errors and flaws are built in and magnify. Problems may lie undetected and not cause any difficulty for years, but then, one day the system collapses as a result of these faults.

Some bureaucracies drown under the weight of their own paperwork and the systems become dysfunctional. They continue to work but in a way that was not intended.

A similar situation can develop in teams. The following verse succinctly illustrates how this occurs.

There are four people named

| Everybody | Somebody |
| Nobody | Anybody |

There was an important job to be done and Everybody was asked to do it.

Everybody was sure Somebody would do it.

Anybody could have done it.

But Nobody did it.

Somebody go angry about that because it was Everybody's job.

Everybody thought Anybody could do it but Nobody realised that Everybody wouldn't do it.

It ended up that Everybody blamed Somebody when Nobody did what Anybody could have done.

3.8   PREVENTING PROBLEMS

Monitoring performance against standards can help prevent problems. We will move to the more practical aspects of the how this can be done in the next chapter. In this chapter we have discussed how standards and objectives can be used to monitor performance. We have concentrated mainly on the ways in which the act of monitoring can be used to prevent or deal with performance problems.

Even though you may wish otherwise, problems do occur and it is only right to be prepared to deal with them in a positive and forward-looking way. If this approach is taken, often the chances of major problems occurring are reduced. Potential difficulties are picked up early and remedial action taken quickly. This means that you and your staff are more inclined and likely to have the energy to devote the time and effort required to improve your operations and developing your abilities.

4

STANDARDS:
CEILING OR PLATFORM?

4.1 INTRODUCTION

In Chapter 3 we looked at how to monitor standards and performance against the achievement of shared objectives. We concentrated mainly on problems and how monitoring can be used to help early preventative or remedial action. In this chapter, we will consider how objectives, standards and monitoring can be used as tools to lift performance and develop skills.

If standards and monitoring are used wrongly they can be seen as indicating the pinnacle of achievement. Normally, most of us, in our everyday work operate at a point somewhere below our maximum. If expectations are set too high, are unrealistic and unrealisable, monitoring becomes a game. The systems and processes are used as weapons by bosses, there to catch out the unwary. This can encourage staff to devise their own systems to get round their manager's system. It can also be a device for unifying the team against its manager.

Used wisely and collaboratively, standards, and monitoring their attainment, can form the basis of a virtuous spiral. This platform, standing on firm foundations, enables excellence to be built. It helps all those standing on it to learn how to learn to do better. Before we discuss ways of creating this sort of environment, which may seem utopian, we will look at the events and behaviour that can impede it.

4.2 WHEN STANDARDS LIMIT PERFORMANCE

Unless everyone is clear from the outset about what is expected and why, standards and objectives can be seen as ideals. They become the ceiling which might be reached by the exceptional few or they may be out of everyone's range. If they are described in terms which are too vague or intangible, people will not be able to translate them into actions. Equally, if the standards are simply the norms, everyday and ordinary, they do not encourage effort or learning. They become the levels of performance expected of the average worker.

Talk of the average can actually be demotivating. What does average actually mean? It can be the mid-point of the full range of items in the sample, or the result of a mathematical calculation in which the values of all the items in the sample are added up and the result is divided by the number of items. With either meaning, there are items above the value of the average and items below. Naturally, no one wants to be just average and certainly no one wants to be below average; we all want to be above average. But to have an average in the first place some must be above, some below and a few in the middle.

Mediocre standards can have the same effect. Most of us do only what we are required to do, and no more. This is not because we are lazy, uncommitted or disinterested in the job, it is because we need to pace ourselves. Our bodies tend to know better than our minds and set internal limits. It saves energy for other activities it finds more beneficial and retains enough energy and brain power left to deal with other aspects of our lives. Doing just enough in this sense is known as 'satisficing'. This term was coined by March and Simon[1] to describe the individual they called Administrative Man, the person who finds a solution to a problem or completes a task in a way that is just good enough, and no more.

In some organisations, this approach purports to be 'just in time' working. Normally this term is used to describe the working practice that keeps stocks at their minimum level. Materials are obtained just before they are needed by the production line.

---

1. March & Simon, *Organisations* (1958).

Likewise, decisions are made when they need to be made, not a minute sooner than is necessary. Sometimes 'just in time' is too late as the approach does not provide slack, or contingencies in case matters go wrong. There is no time to consider alternatives or put in place contingency plans. If the approach is used for managing people, it is possible that putting off matters can be seen as avoiding the issue or worse, prevarication. People matters do not go away, nor do they wait until you have time or the inclination to deal with them. They tend to fester and become more complicated.

In science there is a phenomenon known as entropy. This term can be defined as the inevitable and steady deterioration of a system or society, or as a hypothetical tendency for all matter and energy in the universe to evolve toward a state of inert uniformity. This can happen with people's standard of performance. Even if the standards are easy to attain, they can be seen as the top and out of reach. No one will do more than they need to do to get by, and eventually everyone will sink to the lowest common denominator. The levels of performance will fall as everyone satisfices and things get done, just in time.

If the group regards the standards as being too high, the group will collude to sabotage their attainment:

1. The information needed for monitoring performance goes:
   (a) missing;
   (b) is not collected;
   (c) is falsified.
2. Other things happen to take priority.
3. Standards and expectations, once clear, are misunderstood or forgotten over time.
4. The standards are used to apply only to certain situations.
5. External events or influencers get in the way and prevent achievement.
6. Circumstances change so much that the standards become impossible to achieve.

Standards can also be sabotaged by making the failure to achieve them the responsibility of someone else, often the group's manager – you.

The Hawthorne Studies,[2] even though they were conducted some 80 years ago, are still relevant. The researchers investigating the factors that influenced the performance of groups found that one group had a keen sense of its own identity and had norms, i.e. certain ideas of what was the proper and fair way of doing things. Several of these norms concerned production rate: what was a fair day's work for a fair day's pay? The rate set suited management as well as the workers, but it was well below what could have been achieved without anyone having to make excessive exertions. Another norm was the rule that no one should 'bust the rate' or work harder than the level 'agreed'. No worker should be a 'chiseller', i.e. work at a level below the rate.

Groups can apply pressure on members to oblige them to conform by taking subtle actions. These can include:

(a) kidding rebukes;

(b) hurtful comments and cruel teasing;

(c) playing tricks and jokes on the non-conformist;

(d) having 'private' jokes at the individual's expense;

(e) sending a deviant individual to 'Coventry';

(f) little rewards given when the individual does things right and bigger punishments when the wrong thing is done;

(g) hidden and not so hidden threats;

(h) ostracism – excluding the individual from all group activities and conversations.

These methods of restricting performance are often found in organisations that use bonus or performance-related pay systems. As members of the group are closer to the action and often have time to think about their performance. They will discuss the

---

2. Mayo, *The Social Problems of an Industiral Civilisation* (1945).

standards with their colleagues and know how to 'manage' their output better than their managers, who inevitably have other things to occupy their minds.

Over and above the dynamics of the work group, individuals are able to determine their own work loads. Even though the pressure to conform can be strong, the individual remains free to choose how to perform, regardless of group norms and pressures. Most groups have members who adhere rigidly to the group's standards and conform with their requirements without question or deviation. Others refuse equally strongly to comply. The reasons why they decide to resist the pressure to conform are many. Sometimes the individual disagrees simply for the sake of disagreeing. Others have good reasons for their opinions and their refusal to work to standards. It would be a mistake to discount these, as often the individual will hold their views strongly and care passionately about them. These people are not necessarily easy to manage.

4.3 PEOPLE WHO CARE PASSIONATELY

These individuals are often highly committed to their organisation and their work, sometimes adopting an approach verging on the evangelic. They work very hard, think about what they are doing, and know their business extremely well. They may well be the most experienced, best-informed members of the work group and could easily know more about the job than the manager. However, their views of the standards, the level at which they should be set, what they mean and how to meet them could be very different from yours. Even when they have been involved in identifying and setting the standards, they will have reserved their position and retained the right to disagree. This can leave you in a very difficult situation. There will be no real grounds from which to challenge their position nor will you be able to find fault with their work. The more usual mechanisms of managing performance will not available to you.

The passionate people can be one of the following.

The Social Leader

The individual will have a strong, informal position in the work group. They will command the respect of their colleagues and their opinions will be listened to. Possibly, in the past, they might have held a position of responsibility, for example as shop steward, or they may have attained their leadership role through the strength of their personality. Regardless, they provide an alternative source of power and may easily be a challenge to your authority.

The Angry People

These folk do not agree with you. They think you are wrong-headed and that your ideas are based on bad practice. They believe that you have not taken account of all the relevant factors and are prepared to tell the world exactly what they think. They are vocal and loud, they do not listen and they will not be convinced. They will fight you all the way (even when you are right) and will make life difficult for you till the very end.

Individuals with Strong and Different Views

These people are often members of external groups, such as professional associations, trade unions, or local pressure groups, such as Chambers of Commerce. As well as the organisation's standards to meet, they have allegiance to the objectives of the external objectives. Sometimes, these interests may come into conflict. A common example can be found amongst members of professional bodies which have codes of conduct, statements on ethics, or political stances on certain matters. These interests may be different to those of the employers and have agendas which are in direct conflict with the organisation's strategic plans. An example of this form of conflict can be seen when an organisation makes an application for planning permission to dispose of waste and members of staff are involved in the community group opposing the plan. These individuals' different goals may affect their approach to their job.

Those Reluctant to Change

Some people are naturally fearful of change. It is normal to look for stability and security. Most people are unhappy when their routines are disturbed – everyone likes to have their own cave, warm and safe from attack. They strive to make sure that their environment provides the same degree of comfort. Sadly, the turbulence of the modern world challenges this fundamental part of human make-up. Everyone needs to be adaptable and to be prepared to alter their working practices. Some people take longer than others to understand why this is needed and what it means in practice. They are not necessarily erecting barriers to your plans. In fact, the opposite may be true. If you take time to talk with those individuals, you could convert them, possibly into your greatest allies. We will discuss this group of people again as they form an important yet often misunderstood group.

Those Opposed to Change

Every manager planning a programme of change should think about the ways the affected individuals are likely to respond. If you have a large number of staff, it may be difficult to consider everyone's individual response. It is likely that you will know those who are most likely to disagree with you but have you thought about those who remain silent? Sometimes these individuals are the most difficult to manage. You may not know who they are. They can appear to agree with your plans in public and even offer positive and helpful suggestions. Outside, however, it will be a different matter. They will have the time to think about their opposition and so will be able to put forward arguments that effectively undermine your plans. They will have credible arguments against them and will be able to influence their colleagues. These conversations will be happening outside your purview, possibly in the pub and on the street corner. You may not know who is involved or what is being said.

Those whose Efforts are Misdirected

These people work very hard, doing the wrong things. They may be very good at what they are doing and achieve very high standards. Sadly, they are doing the wrong tasks and the standards are not relevant to the organisation's objectives. Examples of this can be seen amongst trade professionals who have failed to keep up with developments in their occupation. Take the case of the garage mechanic who does a very thorough job. However, he has no interest in catalytic converters and the concern for reducing emissions of exhaust fumes. Car engines have changed considerably, if the mechanic does not learn quickly he will find eventually that there are no cars he can service. Similar examples can be found in all professions, e.g. the barrister not aware of recent judgments, the doctor not aware of advances in the field, the manager who does not appreciate the importance of new safety legislation.

All of these individuals can cause you real problems if you are trying to harness your staff's efforts and focus them on the achievement of common objectives. The processes used for setting standards can help to gain commitment, as we discussed above. The use of relevant indicators to monitor achievement can provide reinforcement along the way. You can also use the standards to establish a climate conducive to continuous improvement and learning.

4.4 CREATING THE CONDITIONS FOR IMPROVEMENT

Continuous improvement is part of Total Quality Management. It stresses that, even when faults have been corrected and the systems are working smoothly, there is still scope for getting better. We have already discussed entropy (natural decay) and, in a competitive environment, unless you are getting better you will be overtaken by others. Without constant attention and polishing, performance levels fall off or become outdated. People slow down and their standards fall. Even the most famous and most admired opera singer has to practice daily and needs regular coaching sessions. The world's greatest footballers know they will not do their best unless they train, keep fit and maintain their skill levels. The same principles apply in business.

People, however, are not able to train and improve under unnecessary pressure and blame. This atmosphere sets up the conditions for a flight or fight response. Fight has been discussed in relation to passionate people. Flight is driven by fear. Fear can be produced through the following.

A Sense of Inadequacy

This is created by a lack of good quality information about performance and the results of one's efforts. If a person feels that their work is just going into a black hole and has no real purpose, eventually they will come to deprecate their own worth. If they are always asked to do only part of a task and are unable to see its place or contribution to the whole, they will feel that they are an unimportant component, a mere cog in the wheel. If they have no contact with the users of their products, they will not know whether they were any good. If they do not know the standards expected, they have no means of assessing the quality of their work nor can they benchmark it against the work of others. They will not know whether they are working well or badly. This will contribute to a sense of worthlessness and inadequacy which in turn leads to low self-confidence and a reduced ability to take control over the situation.

Lack of Information

Horror films and late night television thrillers trade on the human wish to know everything about the universe. There is a basic human terror generated by the possibility of being con-

fronted by 'things that go bump in the night', the things not recognised or understood. In Victorian times, the Sunday sermon,
preaching hellfire and damnation, provided the weekly entertain-
ment and, in giving the comfort of God's grace, the security to
face Monday morning. Many organisations, facing uncertain
futures, present their employees with a view of Hades but give no
hope of salvation. With no information, people speculate and fear
the worst. They tend not to consider a more favourable future.

Uncertainty

The lack of information and creation of pessimist scenarios can
lead to a state of hopelessness. This is compounded if the individuals involved have developed a sense of inadequacy. They get into
a state of depression, unable to apply their energies or think crea-
tively about how to get out of the situation they find themselves
in. They feel that no matter how hard they try, they will make no
difference, the future is inevitable.

Three responses to change have been identified:

1. Deny it will ever happen and carry on regardless.
2. See the threat approaching and work harder doing more of the
   same things. (Everyone knows of managers who work ten or
   twelve hours every day but seem never to achieve anything.)
3. If one is wise, one learns to work smarter. The person thinks
   about what they are doing. They ensure that their efforts are
   directed in the most effective way and are aimed at achieving
   the right things.

If the third stage is not achieved, the result of the second stage is
not salvation but a downward spiral. The individual becomes
more and more exhausted and increasingly ineffective. The more
ineffective, the more depressed and inadequate the individual
becomes and the likelihood of failure becomes greater.

Doubt

As new standards are developed, some people will not be sure that they will be able to meet them. Even people regarded as very competent may doubt their own abilities and be afraid of not being able to achieve what will be expected of them. In essence, they are not afraid of the standards or the unknown. Rather and quite simply, they may be afraid of failure.

Fear of Success

This may seem perverse but some people are afraid of achievement or at least its consequences. Achieving the standards may result in higher standards or more work. Success may bring unwanted attention and recognition. The individuals may find themselves in other groups having left behind existing colleagues.

Loss of the Familiar

Working to new standards may mean the individual has to adopt different work methods or work with new people. Both may require the individual to leave behind well-known practices, colleagues and possibly friends. As discussed earlier, people tend to be naturally conservative and prefer well-known, secure routines. Giving these up can result in a sense of bereavement. This can be almost as intense as the feelings that follow a death. Often the symptoms of this grief and their consequences are not recognised at work. These can have a profound effect on the individual or group's ability to work to the standards normally well within their grasp. We will look at this later. If these factors are duly acknowledged and handled appropriately, it is easier to reduce their negative effects without denying the power and importance of the emotions.

Modern Pressures

Many aspects of modern working life create pressure that is totally unnecessary. The pace of working life, it is said, has accelerated to such a pace that gadgets, such as the mobile phone and laptop computer, are essential pieces of equipment. Decisions have to be made on the run, reports completed on the move, deals struck in railway coaches. How many question the need to work like this? Is the pace real or is it a myth generated by the need to feel important?

The mobile phone provides an example. It is an essential fashion accessory, not only for the young, but also for the middle-aged executive, regardless of gender. Not having one's phone and not being contactable at a moment's notice is seen as a lack of commitment to the job. How is it possible to be effective without a phone? But increasingly using a phone while driving is seen as dangerous for, even with hands-free machines, the lack of attention paid to the road is perilous. The dulcet tones of *Führ Elise* being played by numerous telephones in railway carriages interrupt the clicking of the laptop keyboards and heated debate between important people. The business traveller has replaced the buffet car drunk as the major source of irritation for other travellers, wishing to read and think. To what end? What serious business can be conducted in transit? Perhaps the time would be better spent in reflection, recreation and at peace. The renewed levels of energy would mean that later work effort would be at a higher standard of performance.

Many managers place similarly unreasonable demands on their staff, on each other and themselves. They set and expect unachievable time scales and delivery dates. They make promises they cannot keep and commit other people to doing things without asking whether they are able or willing to comply. They do not accurately assess how long tasks will take. They do not allow for things not working smoothly. They do not have contingencies and stand-bys. They do not plan and they set impossibly high standards.

4.5 BLAME

When standards are not achieved, deadlines pass by and things do not work as well as intended, there is a tendency to look for someone to blame. The rush to the law courts also reflects this trend. We need to find a cause, a person to hold responsible for failures. It seems as though accidents, errors, mistakes and human frailty are no longer possible. Someone must be at fault. Even when the mistake is of our own making, some external cause or failing must be found to explain it. Sadly, explanations alone are not sufficient. They need to be accompanied by retribution and reparation.

This need to hold someone to account is not found only in the law courts. More and more, organisations seem to be following suit. Enquiries and investigations are held to find those responsible and make sure heads roll. Of course, there is fraud, incompetence, negligence and people do deserve to be punished if they do things wrong deliberately. But most of the mistakes are not of this magnitude. Draconian punishment is not the best way of making sure that incidents do not happen in future. Rather the fear of blame and retribution encourages staff to find better ways of covering their tracks and burying their errors. If you want people to be honest about mistakes and learn from understanding what went wrong, you will need to take a long-term view.

Mistakes can be learning opportunities providing you are prepared to create the environment in which staff are not afraid and do not work under shadow of blame. A positive, forward-looking organisation has enough confidence in the honesty of its staff. It is prepared to trust them and give them responsibility for their own actions. They have the authority to take decisions about their own areas of work, having been trained to make them. This form of organisational culture is built on shared objectives and a clear understanding of basic standards. It recognises that the staff's fiercest critics are themselves and that with encouragement and appropriate facilities, they will build from the basics.

4.6   BUILDING A VIRTUOUS SPIRAL: CONTINUOUS IMPROVEMENT

The above statements may seem obvious. No one will deny their worthiness but trying to find examples operating in practice is not easy. How do you go about creating the sort of environment in which standards are seen as the building blocks leading ever upwards? The following steps indicate some actions you can take.

1. **Admit to your own ability for getting things wrong and the need for learning.** This requires insight into your own strengths and weaknesses and a degree of humility.

2. **Encourage your staff.** Give them praise when they do well and point out what was special about their performance. When they could do better give them informative feedback and do not put them down.

3. **Coach your staff.** Demonstrate, and make sure they understand what they are being asked to do. Then follow the nursery rhyme:

   > *I do it normal*
   > *I do it slow*
   > *You do it with me*
   > *Off you go*

4. **Allow for mistakes early on.** Take the risk – they may get it wrong; but they might just get it right. Reduce the chance of errors having a major impact and provide support, but make sure doing the task feels real.

5. **Provide opportunities for practice.** This is the only way to build skills.

6. **Make sure you provide the necessary facilities and resources needed for learning.** Allow for them in plans and budgets.

7. **Build the time needed for learning into doing the job.** Do not allow this corner to be cut. Cutting this part of the plan will decrease the opportunities for deep and long-lasting learning.

8. Ask staff to think about what they are doing by asking awkward questions, such as 'Why?'

9. **Do not regard talking about the job as time-wasting chit-chat.** Encourage purposeful discussion and join in. Conferring with colleagues and developing lines of thought is a productive way to share experience, learn from each other and collaborate on problem solving. The application of several minds can lead to better and more considered ways of approaching the job and solving problems.

10. **Demonstrate that competition can result in everyone losing out.** Show that sharing does not result in anyone giving anything up. Rather it is the way of enabling everyone to win.

11. **Take account of the different ways in which people learn.** Some need to think about their job and take time to read the instruction manual. Some go one step at a time. Others need to get stuck in and learn from experience. Some people prefer to ask someone else for the answer. The ways you prefer to learn and your team members learn interact and react with each other. If you do not respect the difference, you might find that the different styles come into conflict rather than complement each other.

Getting Even Better

Even when the right conditions have been established, standards can slip. We discussed earlier how the brain can easily become lazy. The body is just as lazy. It takes energy and determination to keep physically and mentally fit. When you are under pressure to produce a report, close a sale or respond to complaining customers, it is not easy to find the time to keep up the exercises. Working flat out does not lead to extra fitness but exhaustion. Any athlete knows the importance of balance. Training is planned and the plan includes rest. In management terms, action needs to be balanced with relaxation, reflection and planning the future.

Effective managers make this sort of behaviour part of their normal way of life. They learn to become natural learners. There is a lot of talk about the importance of life-long learning and a growing realisation that for many people school did not work. In their case education was the death of learning. Some people say that they learnt their jobs by attending the 'university of life' but many go from experience to experience without learning anything at all. These people do not get better nor do they stay fresh. At the very best, they stand still. More often than not, they go stale and their minds stultify.

Learning is an activity, an event that may be planned or unplanned. It is also a process. It can be a state of mind:

> *Good better best*
> *Never let it rest*
> *Til your good is better*
> *And your better best*

Of course once you have adopted this way of being, the day you stop learning and getting better is the day you are laid to rest.

Unlocking Potential

As mentioned above, to some people learning equals school, and the memory of school awakens painful memories of inappropriate discipline, punishment and failure. Often the priority in school was to make sure that the children in the class behaved and conformed. The standards used frequently focused on the children's ability to pass exams and on allowing the teacher to have as easy a day as possible. Some argue that learning skills are as natural as walking and talking and it is the formal education system that stops learning as education takes over from play and mimicry. The skills needed to learn how to learn are not expressly maintained and developed. Children are not encouraged to think for themselves or to question what they are being taught. They are expected to do as they are told. To become a life-long learner, the skills of learning how to learn are as important as learning how to read and count. They include:

(a) being able to ask questions;

(b) accepting that a lack of knowledge is not a weakness and not being able to perform a task to the standard of an expert immediately is not a failing;

(c) being humble and not wishing to be best at everything;

(d) accepting that others may know better than you;

(e) being prepared to find out;

(f) being prepared to look foolish as you practise new skills;

(g) being able to laugh at yourself;

(h) reading;

(i) thinking hard about what you have done;

(j) listening to the feedback offered by others;

(k) asking other people for their opinions;

(l) being prepared to contribute to discussion and being willing to share your ideas and experiences;

(m) looking at the ways other people approach similar and different types of job and see if they are relevant to your work;

(n) seeing every day as an opportunity for doing something new or picking up a new idea.

As a manager, you have a responsibility to help other people develop and retain the skills of learning. Not only do you have to make sure that your own working practices involve you in the exercise of your learning skills, you need to make sure that your staff practice theirs. There are several actions you can take to encourage them to flex their mental muscles. These include the following points.

Treat People like Adults

Employers often say: 'People are our greatest resource. We want them to be partners in our enterprise and be involved in decision making.' Yet many organisations treat employees as though they have left their brains at home. Their intelligence is insulted by pretence and half-truths. They are protected from the harshness of commercial realities as though they were children. Their commitment to their employer and job is suspect. If they react to the way they are being treated, they are seen as troublemakers, out to undermine management and not worthy of trust.

The alternative is to accept that employees are adults, with opinions and experiences of their own which deserve to be acknowledged. Their contribution will probably add value to an enterprise. They have as great a vested interest in the future well being of the organisation as the managers. If one person's job goes down, there is a chance that the others will too. It is foolish not to recognise staff's interest and to exclude them. However, if staff are to make a valid and relevant contribution, they need to understand the context in which they are working. Pretending it is too complicated for them to understand and that you are trying to prevent them worrying does not give them or you any credit. It can be seen that you have not explained the situation properly and have failed to involve them appropriately earlier.

Respect Staff's Expertise and Encourage them to Share

One way of demonstrating respect and trust is by recognising how more experienced individuals can contribute towards the development of others. This role does not develop naturally with job-specific skills. Some of the most skilful workers are hopeless at passing on their abilities but some less skilful can make superb trainers.

Some organisations have formalised this role in coaching and mentoring schemes. Mentoring is most often found in management development schemes for trainee managers in larger organisations. Simply put, an experienced manager takes a new starter under their wing and befriends them. They guide them through their early days and provide a testing ground for new ideas and approaches. The mentor provides feedback and guidance without the formality of having to assess performance of the job.

Coaching relates to doing the job. The more experienced worker or manager goes through specific areas of work. Possibly, the coach shows the individual how to do the job. Then, as the individual has a go for themselves, the coach watches, gives feedback and suggests ways of getting better. The more established schemes provide training and support for those in the mentoring and coaching role.

The craft trainer award is given on the completion of a formal training course and the demonstration of on-the-job instruction skills. The on-the-job trainer tends to be found in occupations with a set of specific skills, such as catering, but the approach can be usefully applied in many other areas of work.

National vocational qualifications (NVQ) have led to more opportunities for on-the-job training to take place. Managers and more experienced staff can provide support to those following an NVQ and help them build a portfolio of evidence. Workplace assessors develop the skills of assessing work against the national standards and giving feedback to the member of staff. Before they can perform this role, the assessor has to be able to demonstrate their competence. This involves training and they gain an award that recognises the skills they have acquired and the value of their contribution.

Involve Staff in Planning and Decision Making

There is little point in developing skills and expertise that are not used. Staff know their job better than anyone and will have more information about it than anyone else in the organisation. They will know problems in the flow of work, the quirks of the processes and particular likes and dislikes of the customers. They will have a number of previous experiences from which to draw and mental abilities to apply to solving problems. Excluding them from planning and making decisions about their work denies their abilities. It also reduces their involvement in achieving the objectives and meeting standards. Without their participation, there is only one person with responsibility for the job. That responsibility rests squarely and solely on the shoulders of the manager. Management can be lonely enough without cutting off the very people who should be your closest and nearest allies.

Involving staff in planning does not absolve you from your responsibilities but it does mean that you have a greater pool of abilities, brain power, commitment, enthusiasm and energy at your disposal. Managerial success is often assessed on the manager's abilities to use available resources; be sure to make best use of yours, including those of the human kind.

Ask the Advice and Opinions of Staff

Asking staff for their views is neither a sign of weakness nor an admission of your lack of knowledge. In fact it can be a demonstration of your strength and self-confidence. You can draw on different perspectives and bring in aspects you might not have otherwise considered. No one person can think of everything and cover every angle. Everyone is blinded by their knowledge and limited by their talents.

If you think of solving management problems in the same way as playing a symphony, you will get the drift of this point. The richness of sound comes from the contribution of all the orchestral instruments. The string section cannot reproduce the depth and richness of the brass instruments and the clarity and pitch of the woodwind cannot replace the boom and volume of the percussion. Each section playing alone may be entertaining but together they blend and combine in the partnership of a joint endeavour. Drawing on your staff's advice and views can have the same effect.

Make Learning a Non-negotiable Standard and Include the Assessment of its Attainment as a Part of your Normal Review of Performance

Life-long learning, continuous professional development and the value of being a learning organisation are now seen as important for enduring success. To many of you these may words may smack of good intent, high cost, jobs for management consultants and an erosion of your margins. In the past this may well have been true. There are many charlatans in the consultancy game. The same accusation can be levelled at training.

An investigation carried out by the Training Standards Agency shortly after its formation found that many training providers were not up to scratch. In simple terms, this means that the training was not achieving the results intended. Although there is considerable room for improvement, this does not mean that all training is a waste of time, nor does it mean that training equals learning.

Learning is about thinking about what you are doing, questioning your approaches and investigating how you might do your job better. It means reflecting on how you achieve the results you do and the ways in which you exercise your skills. It requires you to think about how to make improvements. It means talking to your colleagues about their work, giving them useful feedback and asking them for some in return. It means taking risks by trying out different ways of working. Above all it means recognising the need to practise your skills.

A learning company means an organisation that constantly strives to adapt and transform itself. It is also a group of people, working together to improve. As a manager, you are the leader of your staff. In this role you are expected to set the standard and act as the role model. It is your responsibility to require other group members to work to the agreed standard. You are responsible for monitoring performance and working practices and should check for progress. You should also be looking for examples of improvement and achievement.

At the outset, learning should be included as one of the group's explicit norms and a core objective. As a fundamental standard, it should not be open to negotiation or compromise. You should also practice what you preach. Your behaviour and the things you do will be seen by your staff as far stronger indicators of your real beliefs than your words. If you are not engaged in learning and continuous improvement, you can hardly expect your staff to be so. If you reduce your commitment to learning, all other standards will decline and entropy set in.

Celebrate Achievement

There is little, if any, point in having standards if you do not celebrate their achievement. Without constant attention, the standards will be forgotten and, neglected, they will slide into disuse. We discussed earlier the need to eliminate the blame culture and the value of making use of mistakes as opportunities for improvement. Discipline and remedial action have their place and need to be used appropriately. But for reasons that are not immediately obvious, they seem to have taken over from improving performance. The counterbalancing forces of praise and reward get less attention and are often seen only in terms of money.

While monetary rewards are usually welcomed, they can be seen as hollow recognition of achievement, if they are not accompanied by heartfelt thanks and genuine recognition of success. Recognition does not always require whistles, gongs and balloons. Certificates and awards are not needed for everyday success. If they were given out thus, they would quickly lose their currency. Quiet 'thank yous' and the genuine acknowledgement of contribution have greater value than the effort involved in giving them suggests. You will see simple letters of thanks pinned on office walls and they are kept in special places at home. They are remembered for longer than it takes to write them. Remember the saying 'nothing succeeds like success', but if people do not know what success looks like, how can they repeat it in the future?

4.7 SUMMARY

In this chapter, we looked at how standards can be used as platforms from which performance can be improved. They need not be fancy expressions of intent and they do not need great or extra effort. To the contrary, the standards should be closely related to the work you and your staff are engaged on everyday. If standards do not exist, if they are idealistic, or if they are set too high, they will not be useful. They might actually serve to dissuade staff from making the effort needed to attain them.

People do need encouragement to try that little bit extra and keep on doing so. Human beings are naturally lazy and need to keep in training to keep physically and mentally fit. Otherwise, levels of performance will fall off. Standards can be used for learning and continuous improvement. They can support the provision of useful feedback and provide challenge.

If, however, you do not involve your staff in setting the standards, they will not be committed to them and may not be able to relate them to their everyday work. Involving staff will encourage them to be more engaged in what they are doing. This in turn will mean that you will be able to draw on a wide pool of experience and will have more brainpower available. As a team you will be able to learn from your work and plan improvements in your operations. Chapter 5 will explore what happens when you are faced with making these and other changes.

5

PLANNING AND
COMMUNICATING CHANGE

5.1 INTRODUCTION

You agree objectives with your staff and establish standards collaboratively. They are then used by everyone as the basis for improving performance. You monitor achievement, make adjustments, engage in continuous improvement. And everyone lives happily ever after? No. Life is not like that. Things change and even when they say they agree, people change their minds. This chapter will help you deal with those changes and respond in ways that contribute to the development of your own, your staff's and your organisation's performance.

Change can be seen as an inevitable feature of life, to be welcomed and embraced, or it can be seen as a rude interruption, a distraction to be resisted at all costs. The latter approach is one driven by fear, uncertainty and possibly a belief in the absolute truth of the status quo. There are times when it is important to preserve tradition and to learn from the past. The study of history indicates which routes lead to successes and which to failures. If we learn the lessons, we may be able to avoid making the same mistakes without having to go through the same painful learning processes as our predecessors. However, as we have discussed in Chapter 4, hanging on to the past ways of working can lead to decay.

Grasping every opportunity to change is equally foolish. This style of management causes anxiety and insecurity amongst those affected or they quickly learn to ignore the boss's latest bright idea. Managers addicted to change can be said to exhibit the symptoms of promiscuous opportunism and demonstrate a lack of planning skills. If proper planning prevents poor performance, foreseeing and preparing for change are essential. A good manager is able to do this and makes sure all those concerned are well informed of what is likely and unlikely to happen.

We have also referred to the simple fact that staff tend to know their own job as well as, if not better than, their managers. They also are likely to know who is doing what else and where. We will look at ways in which you can make use of your staff's contacts and knowledge and use their intelligence to create alternative views of your future. This will help you prepare for the most probable eventualities and develop a range of suitable responses. This approach helps to reduce levels of uncertainty and the chance of being taken by surprise.

Even if you have involved your staff in the planning processes and talk to them on a daily basis about their jobs and the organisation, there will still be the need for a formal approach to communication. You need to be sure that all members of the team know about critical factors that impact on their jobs. You also need to know that they are keeping each other informed of progress. Your own bosses will want regular progress reports, and other people, outside the immediate circle will probably need to know what is going on. Some communication systems are so complicated that messages get lost in their transmission. Others are so simple everything floods through unfiltered and without a target. We will discuss some of the factors you will need to take into account when developing your communications systems.

Before this, however, we need to consider the nature and degree of change. This will mean that you can design your communications systems to take account of the current situation and any likely changes.

5.2 CHANGE

Change, according to its Chinese symbol, is a dangerous opportunity full of potential and laden with risk. In English we tend to think of it as a short word with one simple meaning. This is false, for the word is used every day to describe a wide range of different types of event. The effects can be of minor significance, affecting only those directly involved in the immediate vicinity. Alternatively, it can be of vast magnitude, involve many people and have major long-term ramifications.

Change can be an evolution, emerging slowly from the current situation and happening so imperceptibily that no one really notices that things have altered. It can be revolutionary, happening quickly and touching everyone. No one can pretend that it has not happened.

Change occurs in different degrees.

First Order

This is when you do more or less of the same things. For example, you find yourself doing more work as your organisation finds new business. If you are in decline or certain areas of work are being stopped, you will find you have less to do on those aspects.

It also happens when plans are altered. A symptom of this type of change can be seen when people complain about the goal posts being moved. It is, of course, possible that these people were not aware of the whole picture and so could only see their area of work, out of context.

Second Order

Sea-change is a popular term used to describe doing things differently. The term comes from Shakespeare's *The Tempest* (I:ii:396-401):

> *Full fathom five thy father lies;*
> *Of his bones are coral made;*
> *Those are pearls that were his eyes;*
> *Nothing of him that doth fade*
> *But doth suffer a sea-change*
> *Into something rich and strange.*

The structures or frameworks remain the same but the substance is dramatically altered. Focus moves from the efficiency of working practice to question the effectiveness of routines and operations. Their contribution to the achievement of the overall objectives is assessed and if they are not thought to be adding value, decisions are made to either substantially revise or eliminate them.

Second order change is more noticeable than first order and has major implications for the people involved and those surrounding them. They may complain of moving goal posts but they are more likely to experience major changes to their working practice, position in the organisation, relationships with other workers or even find their areas of work being no longer required by their employer.

Third Order

Third order change involves the individual or organisation in a fundamental change of direction. It represents a rethink about core purpose. A deconstruction exercise may have been carried out and the key decision makers involved in a period of deep introspection. If the process has been rigorous and searching, the outcome could possibly result in a new statement of mission. There are many examples of senior managers going through such an experience, believing they were engaged on the early stages of third order change. But unless it is followed through, it tends to be an example of old wine in new bottles.

True third order change occurs when you or the organisation come out of the process having undergone some form of transformation, resulting in different values and different ways of behaving. Your previous world will have been turned both upside down and inside out. People talk about going through this sort of transformation after a major upheaval, for example, the death of someone close, or undergoing a life-threatening event. Organisations can experience similar events: a situation that threatens the organisation's survival or a change amongst the key leading personnel after a long period of stability.

The examples in Figure 5.1 describe how the different orders of change could be seen in the development of banking services.

Figure 5.1: Different orders of change in the banking service

First Order	Second Order	Third Order
Local branches	Rationalised locations	Remote locations accessed through technology
Customers known	Mergers, bigger branches, anonymous	Customer first, service quality and flexibility
Paper records	Computerised records not always accessible	Immediate access to information
Available during opening hours	Reduced opening hours	24 hour availability
Narrow range of services	Diversification into finance related business, e.g. estate agencies	Differentiation into small cells of holding organisation Complementary services and partnerships
Emphasis on quality and type of service	Emphasis on cost reduction and uniformity	Emphasis on flexibility, cost effective delivery of services to individuals
Importance of buildings	Importance of efficiency of operation	Buildings irrelevant

Accessing the third order of change is not easy. This perhaps explains why some organisations think they have engaged in this level of change, but, in fact, very little has altered. Some classic examples can be seen in the corporate world. The business pages of newspapers announce a major restructuring designed to address the threats to a company's survival. A few months later the company has to divest itself of key parts. Then a new chief executive is brought in by the board to pull the organisation from the mire.

How do you ensure this does not happen to your organisation? One answer is to ensure that the deconstruction of the current systems and processes is thorough. The analysis needs to go deep enough to uncover the real and root causes of the current situation and problems. Identification of the symptoms alone, although important, is not good enough.

Likewise, the reconstruction needs to be rigorous. A number of alternative solutions should be developed from the diagnosis and their comparative merits explored. The one selected should be the one best able to remove the problems at their root. They should not be the managing director's bright idea, even less should they be the latest idea promoted in the business magazines and Sunday newspapers.

Decision making is often portrayed as a series of choices made on rational grounds. This is rarely the case. People's feelings become involved and intermingled with the facts and figures. Somebody designed systems and introduced processes in the past. They and others have worked hard on their design and may have had to fight battles to get them implemented. They have maintained them and may even tried to improve them. If they are told by a new broom, a young whipper-snapper, the latest fad-monger, that the old ways are not working, are old-fashioned, and or ineffective they will hardly become your greatest supporters.

They will oppose you, argue against you, try to undermine your plans and possibly engage in active sabotage. At the very best, you will leave them insulted, wounded and upset. Even if they go along with your plans for change, they will experience a sense of loss at the passing of the old ways. Recognising this and allowing these individuals time and space to deal with their 'bereavement' gives you a better chance of winning them round. But do not hope to make them enthusiastic advocates for your cause. You may do better by trying to bring them to a state of neutrality.

Taking a participative approach to the development and management of change will help you achieve this objective. If you talk to people about the problems and the reasons for their existence, they will better comprehend what you are planning to do and why. You may also find out about the strength of their sense of ownership of the routines, systems and procedures. By examining their history, you will gain a better understanding of the situation and possibly obtain the respect of those involved. However, this should not tempt you to replicate the previous actions. The intention is to learn from the past and avoid making the same mistakes again.

Exploration of the past should not preoccupy your time, mind or energies. Over-analysis and attempts to allocate blame for past failure should be rigorously resisted. The purpose of the examination of the past is to provide an understanding that will contribute to the development of future proposals and plans. Therefore, as well as listening to those who were influential in the past, it is essential that the people who will be influential in the future are involved. These people are often called stakeholders. These are different from shareholders. A stakeholder is someone with a vested interest in your organisation or area of work. This may include shareholders but, for example, the owner of the newsagency where most of your workers get their morning papers and sweets will be interested in your organisation's long-term survival.

But how do you know who these people are? The following simple guide will help you identify key stakeholders.

Who Knows about the Situation?

1. Who understands the past?
2. Who knows what is going on at the moment?
3. Who is able to foresee what is likely to happen in the future?
4. Who knows enough about how current operations work to understand the possible impact of alternative courses of action?

Who Cares?

1. Who has a stake in the particular area under scrutiny? These people may not be obvious but can play a major role in the success or failure of plans.
2. Who has enough strength of feeling about the area of work or organisation to want to take action (and possibly risks) to improve the situation? You may find that these people have strong opinions about matters!

Who Can?

1. Who has the ability to take the action needed? You will need new and different competencies as your plans will require people to act in different ways. They may require skills other than and different from those acknowledged before.
2. Who has the wherewithal? As well as possessing the skills needed to do the work, people working at the leading edge of change may need the courage to stand apart from the rest of the workforce. They will also need some interpersonal skills to deal with possible conflict.

Moving into the third order of change takes more than just commitment. It needs vision, a sense of the future and a feel for what is likely to happen. These are terms commonly bandied about in management textbooks and we all know that successful leaders are people with foresight and vision. But are these inborn attributes or abilities that can be learnt?

This interesting question requires a book in itself and many great thinkers have already expounded totally different and equally correct views. So rather than enter the debate, let us look at techniques that will help ordinary mortals to achieve the required end-product – a view of the future.

Scenario planning is a process that supports the construction of a number of possible futures. It engages the imagination but aims to develop situations that are realistic and plausible. Once you have created the alternative scenarios, you are able to work out what you need to do to make them. The actions can be broken down, almost into a critical path and you will be able to identify possible obstacles and difficulties.

5.3 GENERATING ALTERNATIVE FUTURES

Stage One

The first stage is to define the parameters that surround your future. We are not concerned, at the moment, with the whole of your life. We all occupy multiple roles and have many areas of interest. If we try to plot possible scenarios for all of them at once, the resulting picture will be too big and complex to deal with. We need to focus on one aspect at a time and then, if needs be, build up the whole from the separate parts. This also helps to give a structure to the world you are trying to imagine. Thus, you could focus on your home life, your career, the future of your particular area of work or profession, your department or your organisation.

You also need a time-frame within which to operate. You should select one that is neither too long or too short. The accepted wisdom is that this should be between ten and twenty years. This may seem a long time, especially since, increasingly, we tend to focus on the short-term. But it can be argued that this has led to some classic failures. Decisions are made for reasons of expediency and can result in precisely the opposite of what was intended.

If you find this sort of time-frame difficult to deal with (there are many things to consider), you may find it easier if you pinpoint specific events that will definitely have happened. These may include passing your 50th birthday, X number of general elections, a new American President, the referendum on joining the euro, the end of petrol fuelled private car, and so forth.

Stage Two

The next stage is to deepen your understanding of the context in which you are operating. To do this you will need to ask the following questions.

1. What are the forces driving change and what are those blocking you from moving forward?
2. Where can these forces be found? They can be identified within your:
   (a) department or section;
   (b) organisation;
   (c) sector?
3. Or they may come from broader environmental sources. Typically these may include:
   (a) political and economic pressures, including changes to legislation and the trends operating in the world;
   (b) sociological and demographic changes, including transforming expectations;
   (c) technological changes: what are the likely (and unlikely) developments on the horizon? What will be obsolete and what could be invented?
   (d) forces from within your sector, including changes of approach and ethos, often engendered as a result of external forces;
   (e) decisions made within your own organisation, for example deciding to move out of an area of business.

4. Who is behind these forces? Some are environmental, coming into existence through the complexity of evolutionary change or another organisation's actions outside your control. Some may be led by individuals whose actions may be influenced.

Stage Three

Once you have gained a good insight into the context and forces at work within your environment, you need to name the key players and stakeholders. Key players need not be stakeholders but they have the ability to influence the actions you take or do not take. They may be aware of their power to determine your future or they may not appreciate the importance of their actions for your future.

Stage Four

You are now ready to create a picture of your future as defined by the parameters you have set. You may find it better to involve the other interested people. But do keep the group to a manageable size – probably about six people. If you want to involve more people, you may like to think about running a series of group meetings so that everyone is able to contribute. Drawing on the work of these groups will allow you to compare the different opinions and build an even richer picture of your future.

When you are in the process of developing the scenarios, be careful not to cut off what may seem to be improbable suggestions at this early stage. Try to avoid writing off ideas before assessing the chances of them happening. People tend to use the words 'never' or 'impossible' too readily. But the impossible does happen; many of the things now taken for granted, at one time were regarded as impossible. If you adopt an open mind and are prepared to accept the unexpected, you are less likely to be taken by surprise.

After all the possible futures have been identified, you need to assess the chances of them occurring. You can do this by giving a weighting or set of odds. This helps to put the most unlikely to one side while you work on the most probable scenarios. It is possible to use words or numbers to define 'chance'.

- **Improbable.** The chances of the event occurring are remote, standing somewhere less than one in a hundred (*odds of a hundred to one*).
- **Unlikely.** The chances of the event occurring are slim, standing somewhere between ten and twenty times in a hundred (*odds of ten to one or five to one*).
- **Unfavourable.** The chances are less likely of the event happening, at 30 per cent (*odds of three to one*).
- **Possible.** The chances of the event occurring are over 50 per cent (*odds of two to one*).
- **Favourable.** The chances are strong, over 75 per cent (*odds of three to one on*).
- **Likely.** The chances of it happening are high, standing at about 80 to 90 (*odds of nine to one on*).
- **Probable.** The chances of it happening are nearly certain, standing at above 90 times in a hundred (*near certainty*).

As the purpose of scenario planning is to develop a number of alternative views of the future, not to predict what will or will not happen in precise terms, you should be careful not to discard the less likely too soon, especially if it is a favoured option. We are not crystal ball gazers but there is always the chance of being able to influence the course of events if we know what to do, or not do, when and increase the chances of it happening.

Stage Five

The next stage is to decide the alternatives on which you want to start doing more detailed work. Choose those which are:

- **most likely:** these will inevitably be contingent because things never happen exactly as we expect. However, the scenarios should be the events you think are the ones most likely to happen;
- **most important:** which of the scenarios will have the greatest impact on your organisation? This impact may be favourable or it may have negative consequences;
- **most favoured:** although personal preference should not take precedent over the other factors influencing the choice of option, it does have a bearing. Ignoring personal opinion drives it underground but it does not eliminate it.

You are now ready to work out what you need to decide and do to make the future happen or not happen. You have the choice and ability to influence events. The term self-fulfilling prophecy describes the situation when your predictions happen. You may be surprised and feel that circumstances have conspire to make them come about, but as Brutus was told in Shakespeare's *Julius Caesar* (I:ii:139-141):

> *Men at some time are masters of their fates:*
> *The fault, dear Brutus, is not in our stars,*
> *But in ourselves, that we are underlings.*

It is not always the forces around you that make things happen or not happen. Coincidences are rare. Change is more likely to be the result of your actions, inactions, responses or lack of response. Regardless of whether they are taken consciously or unconsciously, they can result in the foretold events happening.

We do not exist in isolation. Certainly in organisations, the future depends on collective actions. Involving the key players and stakeholders in the generation of the alternative scenarios is the first step towards obtaining their commitment and active participation in making changes happen. But despite these people's early involvement, there will be many more who need to be brought on board later as the plans unfold.

Their active involvement may vary at different stages of seeing the plan through, and in different ways. Even when they are not directly involved, they will need to be aware of what is happening, if for no other reason than to ensure that they do nothing to inhibit the successful achievement of your chosen future.

The key to gaining the participation of those who need to be actively involved, those whose support is required, and those who need to appreciate what is happening and why is outlined in Figure 5.2.

Figure 5.2: The key to gaining participation

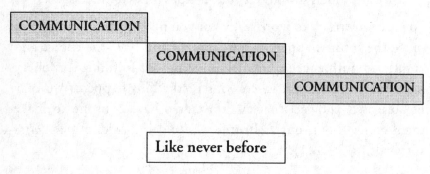

In management texts, communication is often described as a task, to be carried out at specific times in the working week. Weekly updating meetings, monthly team briefing and staff meetings, annual appraisals are all recommended. You are encouraged to review performance every quarter and ensure that the house newspaper is produced every six weeks. Even if you do all of these things and more, formal communications are only the half of the story.

Peter Drucker[1] once described a manager as someone who is accountable for more work than he or she can do alone and so gets some of it done by others. He identified two key areas of work.

---

1. Drucker, *The Practice of Management* (1955).

1. To achieve objectives by making best use of people, materials, money and other resources available.
2. To ensure the future by forecasting, planning, organising, commanding, co-ordinating and controlling.

Thus any manager's success depends on the ability to harness and guide the labour of others and to prepare. If you cannot hope to do all of this alone, the only other option is to gain the active involvement of your staff. The best way of attaining this end is to make sure that everyone understands what is happening and why.

If, however, you approach communications as just a task to be completed at specific points of time, you may make sure that people will know what is happening, but there is a good chance that they will not comprehend. Comprehension is achieved only after a process of exchange and reflection which involves:

(a) the transmission of information;
(b) the chance to ask questions to gain clarity and check the accuracy of the information being received;
(c) the opportunity to discuss the information and consider its implications;
(d) a process of understanding, developing a perspective and generating a response;
(e) possibly a period of disagreement and the comparison of views;
(f) a period of compromise and possible modification of the original message.

The process requires time and commitment. It is hard work and the commitment to high quality communications needs to demonstrate that it is a way of being, more than just a job to be done.

During times of change, especially rapid and radical change, the approach taken can make the difference between well managed successful implementation and a chaotic chain of unconnected events characterised by misunderstandings and confusion. No doubt you have heard the phrase 'they couldn't manage a pxxx-up in a brewery', this is used to describe situations in which the managers are seen to be doing different things. They do not appear to know the overall plan and don't talk to the people affected. Planning the communications process, making sure that succinct messages are delivered to the right people at the right time, and that they are properly understood can prevent this.

5.4   EFFECTIVE COMMUNICATION

Effective communication is not about telling everyone everything all of the time. This is information overload. *Effective communication is ensuring that people have the information they need, in a form they can understand, when they need to know it.*

Let us deconstruct this sentence to be clear about our meaning.

The People

Decide who needs to know what. It may help to think again of the key players and stakeholders. Having identified them you can assess their proximity to and their degree of active involvement in the changes. Those most closely involved in the implementation and those most affected are the people who need to know the most, the soonest. You may find that these are two distinct groups of individuals. Those involved in enacting the plans may not be those whose work and jobs are affected by them.

For example, the people involved in data inputting following the installation of a new computer system will be affected but they are unlikely to be involved in specifying the operating system. Their interest is more likely to lie in the layout of the office and work stations, and they will have views on operational aspects such as short cuts and sequences of work-flow.

If the key players or stakeholders are groups, it can be worth thinking about the particular needs of individuals within them. Everyone absorbs information at different rates and has different concerns and priorities. Change, even when it contains the most exciting and promising opportunities, holds elements of danger and risk. Therefore, when planning how to communicate your plans, you need to remember that your audience will comprise a number of individuals, possibly with very different interests and needs.

The actions you can take to make sure that the communication process is of high quality include:

1. **Ensuring that the information is not distorted during the transmission of the message.** This means checking that the people intended to receive it did so, fully and accurately.

2. **Giving your staff the chance to ask questions.** This will help them gain clarity and help you check the accuracy of the information they have received.

3. **Providing your staff with the opportunity to discuss the plans.** The most common thought that first springs to mind when given the news of change is: 'What does this mean to me?' As soon as the individual starts thinking about this and tries to find the answer for themselves, they tend to stop listening to what else is being said. There is therefore a very real chance that they have missed important parts of the plans that you know you have told them.

    The 'busy-ness' of their minds will also provide opportunities for misunderstanding and getting hold of the wrong end of the stick. You need to be prepared for this and be ready to go over the essential parts several times, if needs be.

4. **Giving them time after you have given them the information so they can discuss what you have told them and consider the implications.**

5. **Respect the fears, concerns and worries of each individual.**

6. **Some people will be quite happy to express their initial thoughts openly, in a group meeting, others will prefer to consider what is being proposed.** They might appreciate an opportunity to discuss their reaction and thoughts with you privately. People often believe that their questions or anxieties may seem silly to other people so they are unhappy to

reveal them publicly. Nevertheless, to the individual concerned, they are real and important. The individual deserves the time they need to put things into perspective and get the answers to specific questions. This will help them identify the real issues and separate out those that are imaginary or without foundation.

7. **Allowing a period of disagreement, if needed, and encouraging the comparison of views.**

8. **Enabling a period of compromise and, if required, modification to the original message.**

9. **You may find that if you do not invest the time needed for the above stages, individuals' anxieties grow and get out of all proportion to reality.** If this happens, you may find that, in the long run, the amount of time needed to rectify the situation is considerable and the process more painful.

10. **Dealing with shock and a sense of bereavement.** Even at a time of growth and advancement, there will be parts of the present that will be left behind. People develop routines and affection for the things they do every day. To an outsider, these may seem irrational and prosaic, but human beings are creatures of habit and are reassured by the familiar.

11. **Handling disagreement and conflict.** It may be a surprise to you to find that your plans do not meet with universal approval. The chances are that you have been working on them with like-minded people. You probably think that you have thought of all the potential problems and found ways of dealing with the difficulties. It is not unreasonable to expect that, when you make the plans public, everyone should agree wholeheartedly, just unrealistic.

Dealing with Conflict

You may be shocked to find that some of your staff do not like your ideas to such an extent that they are prepared to publicly oppose them and you.

If you plan how you are to deliver the message and think about who will be receiving it, you can anticipate who will object to your proposals and consider their reasons. You can even plan how to deal with the most predictable areas of conflict and be ready to deal with the unpredictable – for, no matter how well prepared you are, something will inevitably arise. If you know your staff well, this is not difficult. If you are dealing with a large group, you may well be wise to take advice from those who know the members of the group better than you.

The test of a good manager is how opposition and conflict are handled. Some managers find any form of conflict abhorrent. They cannot cope. They avoid arguments by running away from them or pretending everything will be alright in the end. They fudge disagreements and smooth over troubled waters. Some, ostrich-like, bury their heads and insist the conflict does not exist. They hope that, by ignoring it, it will go away.

Nothing is further from the truth. Buried conflict thrives on the lack of attention. It grows and transmutes and bubbles below the surface, occasionally erupting in so many different forms so that it is nearly impossible to trace the root cause. A different approach is to acknowledge the areas of conflict in the early stages; be open about them, take appropriate action to deal with the issues at source before they can grow and become complex.

Other managers see questioning and challenge as tests of their authority and almost a personal insult. Rather than seeing these as symptoms of conflict, a different approach is to see the questions and challenges as tests of your plans. The detailed questioning and 'what ifs' will examine the robustness of your proposals. Discussing possible areas of future difficulty can be a way of ensuring that potential problems are dealt with before the plans are too far on the road. The collective brains, although they may initially seem hostile, can produce better solutions. This approach also helps to involve people actively and will help them gain understanding of what is being proposed.

When thinking about the likely responses to change, we often think about those directly involved and perhaps those on the edge of the plans. How often do we consider the people who may be touched by the proposals but not immediately affected? The following people may have the power to make the difference between success or failure.

Your Boss

In so many organisations, for some strange reason, the different levels of management see each other as the enemy. Typical assumptions include:

...the idea that staff:

(a) are against change;

(b) are incompetent;

(c) will not agree;

(d) will not understand;

(e) are not interested;

...and that bosses:

(a) are incompetent;

(b) are only interested in feathering their own nests;

(c) will steal their staff's ideas to make themselves look good;

(d) will knife their colleagues in the back given half a chance;

(e) will side with those against their staff;

(f) will blame their staff if things go wrong;

(g) will take the credit if things go right.

No wonder life in many organisations is stressful and progress difficult!

Your boss should be your best friend, the person with whom you can talk through ideas before they even get to the planning stage. There should be no secrets and no surprises. Your boss is there to help you do your job and develop your abilities. This can be achieved through the following four areas.

1. **Challenging**. Asking you to explain your ideas in detail and posing awkward questions such as:

   (a) have you thought of X ?

   (b) what will you do if Y happens?

   (c) how will you handle P if they do not agree with you?

   These are not intended to put you on the spot. Rather, they are being asked to help you anticipate possible problems that you may not have thought about.

2. **Coaching**. Many of the situations encountered in management are not new. Some are, but others are likely to be recurrences of those that have arisen before. It is possible that it is you who is new to the problem, rather than the problem being new to everyone. The boss's job is to be able to distinguish between those which are genuinely unfamiliar to everyone and those which are simple rehashes of previous situations. The boss is there, with the benefit of their previous experience, to help you manage the present situation.

   Coaching demands that past experience is shared in a non-directive way. The coach does not tell you how to do it good. The coach:

   (a) makes suggestions;

   (b) encourages you to have a go;

   (c) tries to reduce dangers but leaves enough risk for the trial to be realistic;

   (d) supports practice, essential for skill improvement;

   (e) gives feedback designed to give information from which you can reflect on your experience;

   (f) allows you to develop your own approach.

3. **Mentoring**. The boss can only act as your mentor if the relationship between you is right. Mentoring is different from coaching. The mentor's interest extends beyond the job or a particular task. The mentor focuses on your long-term development and wider role. The concern is how you, as a person,

are approaching your job. The mentor's role is to help you work through, possibly for yourself, any situation or challenge you may be finding difficult. The mentor does not necessarily provide advice or answers, though sometimes this might be appropriate. Sometimes, the mentor does nothing more than listen, very actively.

4. **Providing new information and experiences.** The boss can help you extend your body of knowledge and experience by:

    (a) passing on an article from a trade journal or newspaper;

    (b) pointing you in the direction of a website;

    (c) asking you a difficult question and sending you to find out the answer;

    (d) lending you a book;

    (e) discussing a news item from the television, radio or newspaper.

    Your boss may suggest that you:

    (a) talk to a colleague;

    (b) visit a customer or supplier;

    (c) get involved in a community or charity activity, such as those offered by Business in the Community;

    (d) attend a training course;

    (e) take the lead on a project that will involve you in a new area of work.

These are not designed to give you a hard time. They are learning opportunities from which you will develop your ability to perform your role in its broadest sense. They will also prepare you for future challenges and give you experience of techniques that you can use to help, in turn, with your staff's development.

If you and your boss are able to establish a relationship based on trust and openness, you will find that you are able to learn from each other. The relationship will reach a level of maturity where future plans can be discussed in a non-critical way. This does not mean that your boss should not criticise your proposals.

But that criticism will be 'critiquing', in other words, looking for the plan's weak points (not yours) before it is cast. The possible outcomes are explored and potential difficulties examined. Perhaps it would be better to call this phase of planning change a pre-operational review. The purpose of this is to hone the final plan and test it before presenting it to a wider audience.

If things do go wrong, your boss will have been involved from the very beginning. You will both have a good understanding of why certain proposals were made and the reasons behind their inclusion in the plan. You will not have to spend time briefing your boss, explaining and having to justify your decisions after the event. You will be able to concentrate on the current situation and work together on how to resolve it, hopefully before too much damage has been done. Your boss should be your supporter not your opponent.

Other Stakeholders

Who else should be involved in the early stages of your plans? Who are the key players and stakeholders? Their interest may not be direct or overt but you may find, that without their support, your plans could come to naught. They may have the power to influence or even control the situation around you.

Key players and stakeholders may be in groups or individuals.

1. **Managers of other sections who are affected indirectly by your plans.** You may not have recognised the likely impact on their area of work as it might be outside the scope of your operation. How will the finance department, for example, be affected by the discussions you are having with your customers to speed up the time from order to delivery? Will it mean that the finance staff will have to produce invoices in a shorter space of time?

2. **Members of the board or governing body who may have a particular stance on a strategic or policy matter.** For example, if you are planning to bring in agency staff rather than appoint

employees to cover a new project, you will need to answer how this will help implement the organisation's commitment to equality of opportunity and the achievement of the Investors in People award.

3. **Staff representatives or trade unions.** These often have a structure that mirrors your organisation's structure. Will your plans for reorganisation affect their internal working arrangements?

4. **Customers who may have good working relationships with individual members of your staff or have bolted your systems onto their own.** Will your plans disrupt the relationship or mean they have to change their internal processes?

5. **Suppliers who may have worked your requirements into their operations.** If you change your working patterns, for example by reducing your stock levels but increasing the frequency of orders, will this create turmoil for their work planning?

Figure 5.3 may help you consider who the key players and stakeholders and determine the extent of their influence over the success or failure of your proposals.

Figure 5.3: Key players and stakeholders

Competitors	Potential competitors
Your governing body	External regulating authorities (e.g. Health and Safety Inspectors or the bank)
Existing customers	Potential customers
Your boss	
Immediate colleagues	Other peers and colleagues
YOU	
Your staff	
Your colleagues' staff	Staff in other sections
Your suppliers	The organisation's suppliers

Making Friends and Influencing People

The following tips may help to win the key players and stake-holders over to your side and make them support your proposals. This does not mean that they will agree with everything you suggest. That is not the idea. The intention is to ensure that they do not oppose you from a position of ignorance. They may challenge you and oblige you to confront thoughts and opinions your would prefer to ignore. But this is to ensure that you have considered potential obstacles and included them in your contingency planning. The ultimate and, hopefully, shared goal is to increase the chances of your plans working.

Consider the following.

The Information They Need

1. What do they *need* to know?
2. What do they *want* to know?
3. What *should* they but perhaps would rather not, know?

The Content of the Message

The message may need to be packaged differently for different audiences, particularly if its contents are sensitive. However, the main thrust of the message should be the same for all members of the wider audience. You should not put yourself in the position of being accused of speaking with forked tongue, giving preferential information to one group or individual over another, misleading people or telling only part of the story.

If you plan the content of your message in detail for each audience, you will prevent this happening. Identify the key points and separate them from background or supporting information. Remember that the first question in many people's minds will be 'What does this mean to me, how will I be affected?' This will help you frame the contents for each audience while retaining the necessary consistency.

Your message, regardless of audience, should be:

(a) succinct;

(b) to the point;

(c) in plain English.

How the Information is to be Transmitted

You should consider the mode of delivery you are going to use for each audience. Although the content will be the same, how you present it will influence how your audience will receive it. Information technology has made sophisticated programmes that can create whizzy presentations freely available to any one who can use a keyboard and mouse. But the detail on the screen, the speed of delivery, the music and graphics can draw attention away from the main purpose of the presentation – the actual message. Remember the adage: the medium is not the message.

When deciding how you ought to deliver your message to each and every audience give thought to the following questions.

1. Which medium is the most appropriate for each audience?

2. How will the medium reinforce your message?

3. How will the medium engage the different senses? Will it aid comprehension through sight, hearing, touch, smell, if appropriate and possibly experience?

When to Deliver your Message

Consideration should be given to who needs to know about your plans first, then second, and who should be the last to know. Even when careful attention is given to the initial stages, you can easily neglect to consider how those at the end of the line will react to their position. There is a good chance that they will find out from those who were told before them. What are you going to do to ensure those receiving the message later will be told what you want them to know before you are able to tell them yourself? If you don't know the answer to this, you may have to spend a long time correcting wrong impressions and smoothing down people who have been needlessly upset.

On the other hand, if you tell people too soon, they may not be able to grasp the relevance of your message and its implications. You could then be faced with a situation in which you believe you have taken reasonable steps to communicate your plans and ensure that people are briefed properly, but they respond by saying that they didn't know, they had forgotten, they didn't appreciate what you meant, and so on.

If you leave it too late to tell them about your plans, you could be accused of not giving people enough time to think about what you are suggesting. They may want to give a considered response, which could give rise to some important issues that you have not addressed. But the shortage of time prevents them from thinking about and discussing your plans. All they can give you is knee-jerk reactions and comments made hastily without proper thought. These in turn lead to misunderstandings and conflict. Rather than get into such no-win situations, you can avoid them by planning when to inform the separate groups.

You can also ensure that the delivery is appropriately timed. This means thinking about when in the day your message stands the best chance of being received accurately. What hour of day? What point in the week or in the work cycle will be the best? How are they likely to react? How will this affect their work? Will production or the quality of customer service suffer? It is likely that people will want to talk about your proposals, especially if your message has been controversial. Is time available and are you ready for this?

The Messenger

Who is the best person to tell each group? You do not always have to be the one to convey the message.

1. A member of your staff who has been involved in the planning may be the person best placed to tell his or her colleagues.

2. Your boss may be the best person to start the presentation to the Board and then hand over to you so you can outline the detail.

3. The sales team may be able to tell their customers what they need to know better than you.

4. The purchasing manager may be able to make sure the suppliers understand how the changes will impact on them.

Where to Tell People

If you want to tell all your staff at one time, is there a big enough venue available? If not, how are you going to tell them? If you hold two or more sessions, what will the people who attended the first say to those coming to the last? Will the message get distorted and the temperature increased?

Make sure enough time is allowed. There is no point in trying to save minutes and end up rushing the meeting. It will be a false economy, for the time saved will be needed, plus more, to rectify misunderstandings. There will also be outstanding matters to be dealt with. These may have been simple details at first, but being left, they can develop into important issues or possibly points of principle.

It is not uncommon to find that, for example, when you are invited to present to senior managers, you may be allowed a ten-minute slot on their packed agenda. If you know you cannot deliver the message accurately and fully in that time, say so right at the beginning. You can do nothing worse to a set of plans than to transmit them in a rushed, incomplete fashion. You will not do justice to your proposals or yourself if you find your audience is shuffling papers, thinking about the next item on the agenda or are aware of running late for their next meeting.

Consider:

1. When does each stakeholder *need* to know about your plans?

2. When *should* each stakeholder be told about your plans? This should not be too soon to be irrelevant; nor so late that people cannot grasp the full implications of the message and formulate a considered response.

3. How is each stakeholder likely to react?

4. When is the best time to tell them and in which venue should they be told?

5. Who should be told first?

6. Who will be last to know and how will they respond to being last?

7. What do you need to ensure that the grapevine is not mischievous and does not contain misinformation?

Check Understanding

Before you leave your audience, regardless of their seniority, you should provide them with a summary to reinforce the main points of your message. It may be appropriate to prepare a written summary of the key points – but if you do, make sure you have enough copies for everyone.

If possible check your audience's understanding of these key points. A good way of doing this is by posing key questions. This technique should be used with caution and can be dangerous, especially with large groups. At the very least, you should allow your audience the chance to ask questions. You should prepare for this by anticipating the most likely questions. But you should also be ready for the unexpected.

5.5 SUMMARY

This chapter has examined the processes of communication and methods of dealing with change. We looked at the levels of change and discussed the need to engage the third level, if you want to ensure that fundamental changes to ways of working and attitudes occur. We also considered who to involve at which stage of planning the change programme.

We outlined a way of developing alternative plans so that you can decide which option is the most likely and the most feasible to implement. We finished by considering the communication process and who to tell, what and when. We will next discuss what happens when you begin to implement the plans. People will be asked to leave behind their known ways of working and possibly work colleagues. They will be asked to learn new methods and possibly adopt other ideas. How well you manage this critical stage will affect the long-term success of your plans.

6

DEALING WITH ENDINGS
AND BEGINNINGS

6.1 INTRODUCTION

Rarely is managing people's performance about doing the same thing, time after time. Yet maintaining levels of performance and assuring quality are important parts of any manager's job. Making sure that people can sustain their interest year on year and continue to produce quality takes skill, especially if the jobs are highly repetitive and boring. However, these types of jobs tend now to be the exception rather than the rule. In most jobs, and for most people, some aspect or another will change.

We will take a slightly different approach to this subject than that found in many management books. Often you are offered guidance on how to deal with the tasks required to make the changes. You are told about the things to do, the way to manage the project, and sometimes, how to manage the people involved. Some books cover the processes and underlying dynamics of the situation. Few deal with the organisational equivalent of bereavement. We will cover this topic by considering what needs to be done to let go of the well-known routines embodied in the status quo. Moving on inevitably means leaving something or someone behind. Acknowledging the feelings involved helps to make the process positive and forward looking. It also helps to prepare people for the new ways of working and new ideas. However, if the process is characterised by fear and a reluctance to let go, it is hardly likely to be conducive to learning new routines.

Working patterns can become familiar and comfortable and the social relationships developed over time can have strong emotional bonds. Essentially human beings are social creatures and work is a social activity. Even those individuals who prefer their own company engage in pleasantries and social interactions. Most of us need contact with our fellow beings at some point of the day and most days we are at work. The relationships we build are based on mutual affection and shared interests. Many firm and long-standing friendships grow at work. Some relationships have no emotional foundations, the parties may not even like each other, but even the people we dislike become familiar and part of the scene.

Organisational change can disrupt relationships and the daily vista. Breaking the links between people can generate an emotional response not expected when you are preparing for implementation. It is not easy to plan for emotional responses as they can be unpredictable. Nevertheless, you should consider the implications your plans will have on people's whole being and life in the organisation.

In discussing these considerations, we will look at some actions you can take to help people continue to perform their jobs well during periods of change. We have already discussed the importance of talking to people, involving them in planning the new ways of working, gaining their views of the implications of the change and taking account of their opinions. The importance of the communication chain can not be over-stressed. Communication, as we discussed in the Chapter 5, is more than simply telling people what you intend to do to them. It means ensuring that they have time to ask questions, think and understand and respond to your proposals. But even then it does not stop. To convince your staff you are serious about respecting their views you need to be seen to act, appropriately on them. Thus a chain is developed (see Figure 6.1).

Figure 6.1: The communication chain

When things go wrong, so often the wail of regret is 'if only I had known of *that* before'. Often '*that*' was known by someone and that someone is usually heard to say, 'Well, if only they had asked me, I could have told them about *that*.' Equally common is the claim, 'I tried to tell them *that* wouldn't work but they are not interested in my opinion.'

6.2 LOST PRACTICES AND ROUTINES

Human beings are creatures of habit. We learn routines quickly, frequently without realising that we are learning them. This ability is acquired very early in life. New parents are advised to settle their offspring into a regular pattern quickly, to maintain it and avoid unnecessary disruption to the young child. We surround ourselves with little rituals that guide us through each day and prepare us for the next. Generally, we know what to expect and draw on previous experience to enable each event to be managed smoothly with the minimum of energy or excitement – or, at least, most people are like this. The centuries over which we have evolved have not affected some people as much as others and have left them with love of danger. While they may have retained the wish for a challenge and thrill, most of us would prefer to miss the exciting prospect of meeting a sabre-toothed tiger on a daily basis. We prefer to have our world a little bit more controlled and the hazards reduced to manageable proportions.

We like to know what our world contains, what is likely to happen next, how other people are likely to behave and what outcome is likely to result. Some of us look to the stars to predict the future, others read the runes, which may be able to forecast the performance of the stock market, the form of the runners in the 2.15 at Sedgefield or the messages hidden between the lines of the boss's last memo. We ask others who we believe are more knowledgeable than ourselves for their opinions, and we anticipate. Most of the time we are right and the future contains no surprises. Little changes as we continue to reinforce our daily routines and pattern of life.

We do this without realising fully what we are doing. But every little experience adds a further layer to the patina which covers our view of our world and the people in it. The experiences do not need to be new; more of the same acts just as well to consolidate previous learning and confirm existing beliefs. Gradually, the patterns of behaviour and ideas that form the patina become hardened and become part of our being.

This is not a bad thing. We are born with very few abilities. Even innate talents need to be used and refined before they become fully developed. The vast majority of our skills and abilities are grown from years of practice. We are taught and influenced by the key people in our lives – family members, teachers, friends – and increasingly we are exposed to ideas of others outside our immediate circle. Our belief systems become established and our ideas honed through questioning and experience. Rarely are we required to examine the whole of our portfolio of skills and attitudes. Most of the time they are accepted for what they are – pieces of the very complex three-dimensional jigsaw that is the individual. We can assess ourselves and others on a superficial level. Even the most sophisticated psychometric device claiming to reveal the whole truth about an individual's personality can only scratch at the surface manifestations – if only for the very simple reason that still we do not fully understand personality and how the human mind works.

Two Americans, Jo and Harry, developed a simple model in the form of a matrix. The JoHari Window shows how greater insight into ourselves and others can be gained by pushing back the cross bars that divide the known from the unknown (see Figure 6.2).

Figure 6.2: The JoHari window

SELF

		Things I know	Things I don't know
OTHERS	Things they know	*The Arena*	*The Blind Spot*
	Things they don't know	*The Facade*	*Total Unknown*

Insight

The model in Figure 6.3 describes how our talents become buried in our subconscious.

Figure 6.3: How talents are buried in the subconscious

Unconscious incompetence
(I do not know I cannot do something)

Conscious incompetence
(I know I cannot do something)

Conscious competence
(I can do something slowly and not very well)

Unconscious competence
(I do not know that I can do something)

Once we become proficient in an area of work or particular skill, we tend to lose our appreciation of its complexity and any difficulty we experienced while learning the skill. Many of our skills are learnt early in our lives. For example, most people acquire most of their reading skills by the age of ten. Ask anyone to describe how they read and they will have some difficulty in describing the process to you. Ask them how they learnt to read, the chances are you will get a blank look.

The reason for this is that, for most people of normal abilities and intelligence, even highly complex skills become routinised into the mental and physical activities we do every day without thought. Can you remember learning to drive a car? Do you recall the difficulty of getting your feet, head and hands to work independently while you judged the speed and distance of other vehicles coming at you – from in front, the side and from behind. At the same, time you would probably have been listening to your instructor's voice while worrying about the possibility of a child running from the pavement. The process of learning how to drive results in all of these things being melded into the one task – getting to work safely, etc. As you become more competent and practised you will probably add a few more tasks into that time – such as planning the order of the jobs you need to complete during the day. If you approached driving as if it were a brand new task each time, you would find that the demand on your mental capacities and energy would leave little space for the other activities. There is always the chance that in forcing your skills back to the conscious will take your level of competency back as well.

We routinise tasks so that some inner resources are left free. They are needed in reserve to deal with those matters we cannot anticipate. The chances of the unexpected happening may be low, but there is always the possibility of finding the modern day equivalent of the sabre-toothed tiger in the filing room.

Once a pattern of behaviour, a group of ideas and a corresponding set of values become embodied in an individual's daily routine, it is very difficult to untangle them and understand where they have come from and why. The patina forms a part of the rich fabric whose weave creates the unique individual. If you look at how you behave, question why you hold the beliefs you do and try and work out where each originated, you will find that you are trying to unravel a multi-layered, many-coloured three-dimensional being.

Some parts will be tangible, others misty, ever moving and slipping from your view. Some may seem to contradict each other and appear irrational when subjected to scrutiny. You may even find that, on later consideration, some of the ideas you have held for a long time now appear to be out of date and irrelevant. But you may not have revised them earlier simply because you have not thought about them. You may not have had any reason to reconsider their worth. They will have remained in vaults of your mental bank, just lying dormant. Nevertheless, they are familiar and, along with the corresponding patterns of behaviour, comfortable habits.

Generally speaking we do not like to change our habits. Even the most risk-seeking individuals who thrive on the excitement of challenge and the unfamiliar, need some degree of stability and points of reference. Maslow[1] described a hierarchy of needs which shows how we depend on the satisfaction of the most basic needs before attention can be given to the ones at the higher levels (see Figure 6.4).

Figure 6.4: Maslow's hierarchy of needs

Physiological	The need for food, drink, shelter, warmth and relief from pain.
Safety and Security	The need to feel safe and secure.
Social and Affiliation	The need for friendship and interaction with others.
Esteem	The need for self-esteem and the esteem of others.
Self-actualising needs	The need to fulfil oneself by maximising the use of one's abilities, skills and potential.

1. Maslow, *Motivation and Personality* (1954).

Maslow argues that it is only possible to move into the next level when the preceding needs are satisfied. The self-actualised person is attributed with fifteen characteristics.

1. More efficient perception of reality and more comfortable relations with it.
2. Acceptance of self and of others.
3. Spontaneity.
4. Problem centred.
5. Detachment: the need for privacy.
6. Autonomy: independence of culture and environment.
7. Continued freshness of appreciation.
8. Mystic experience or the oceanic feeling (i.e. feelings of limitless horizons, opening up to the vision).
9. Social interest.
10. Deep interpersonal relations often with few rather than many individuals.
11. Democratic character structure.
12. Discrimination between means and ends.
13. Sense of humour.
14. Creativeness.
15. Resistance to enculturation (i.e. able to get along in the culture but remaining detached from it).

There has been some debate about the accuracy of the hierarchy. It is known that people risk or reject the satisfaction of the lower levels to attain greater heights. Nevertheless, it serves to remind us that people cannot operate effectively nor achieve their full potential if their basic needs are under threat or prone to be changed.

How often do we threaten our people's safety and security when we plan organisational change? We place the future security of their livelihoods under threat and raise the following questions in their minds.

1. Will there be a place for me?
2. Will my ability to earn be affected?
3. Will my level of income be reduced?
4. Will my location change?
5. Where will my desk be placed?
6. Will the new office be as warm, light, spacious?
7. Where will I get my coffee?
8. Will I have to move location completely – how will that affect my family?

We threaten the social groups with reorganisation plans.

1. Will I be moved into another work group?
2. What will happen to my colleagues and friends?
3. Will the lunchtime badminton sessions be disrupted?
4. Will I like my new colleagues?

We undermine people's self-esteem by:

(a) removing tasks they were well able to do;
(b) introducing tasks they can not do;
(c) training not always being made available;
(d) not always giving due recognition to previous expertise.

Psychological Reaction

Even when changes to work practice are relatively minor, they can cause people to experience a psychological reaction. Often this is seen as resistance and opposition rather than a normal response. Treating people's reactions as if they are negative and unhelpful can make matters worse. Introducing a new task or routine can, in effect, strip your staff of their abilities. Inevitably, they will have to stop or change their normal way of working to create space for the new task. In taking away their routines and replacing them by behaviours and thoughts they do not know, you are taking them from being unconsciously competent back to being consciously incompetent.

Consider the following example: XZX Company, an insurance company, decided to replace the switchboard with a new computerised system that would give direct dialling into each extension and provide voice-mail facilities. After Easter, everyone would have a new extension number. The reason behind the decision was to reduce the amount of time spent by customers in getting hold of a member of staff. However the hidden implications were:

(a) incoming telephone calls had previously been screened and directed by the switchboard staff to the right person. In future staff would have to greet callers and comply with the company's standard phraseology;

(b) if they were not the person the caller wanted, they would have to refer calls to other extensions and prepare callers to leave messages on the voice-mail, if the person they wish to speak to was not available;

(c) the chances of calls being wrongly directed would increase and members of staff would find themselves dealing with customers who were lost in the system;

(d) no one would know the new extension numbers. For a while everyone would have to use the directory until they remembered the new ones;

(e) everyone would have to learn how to use the voice-mail system;

(f) the switchboard staff, although some were still needed, were uncertain about their future;

(g) staff and the remaining switchboard operators would have less contact with each other.

Meanwhile, the manager of the motor insurance department decided that it was time to change the way in which the internal management information was stored and reported. His son had just bought a new computer system, which included a graphical package. The manager was duly impressed and decided that the monthly targets would be easier to understand if they were presented pictorially rather than in tables. He decided that, in future, everyone would keep their records on a computer database rather than the paper record sheets.

Everyone thought the existing system was easy. Each day, they recorded the number of renewals, new enquiries, new policies issued, new claims and claims settled. At the end of each week, the team leaders collated their team members' daily sheets and gave the summarised information to the manager's secretary who then produced the monthly table. This showed activity levels month by month against targets and allowed the cumulative annual situation to be seen as trend lines. Everyone understood it and knew what to do and when to make sure the information was accurate and up to date.

The manager wanted more graphs and in colour. Everyone would need to learn how to use a new database so they could each directly input their own figures. The team leaders would still have to pull off the figures for their own group and the secretary would still have to produce the monthly figures, but the manager was convinced that it would be better.

The hidden implications were that:

(a) staff would also be using their computers for their voice-mail and to find telephone numbers as well as accessing the customer and policy information programme;

(b) they could either record each activity on paper and transfer the figures on to the database later or record them directly onto the database as things happened during the day;

(c) if they did the latter, they would have to toggle from the client and policy programmes back and forward to the database;

(d) many of the computers were at the edge of their capacity and were increasingly crashing, when excessive demands were placed on them.

On top of the internal changes, the industry regulator had decided to issue new quality checks to ensure that customers were being properly advised about the detail and costs of their policies.

A standard checklist had been produced and all renewals and new policies had to be compared to the standard. Customers were to be asked to complete the checklist on receipt of their policy and return it signed. In future, it would not be possible to close a file until the document had been received. Obviously some system to chase up non-returns was needed.

One of the most experienced members of staff in the motor insurance department was due to start maternity leave at the beginning of June, but her work would not be covered. One of the four team leaders was shortly to move into the life department. A promotion for one of the clerks was in the offing and it was expected that a new trainee would then be appointed. Many policies were due for renewal in the summer because, until the new registration date had been introduced in 1999, many customers bought new cars around August – and the holiday season was approaching. The manager could not understand why, when he went in one Monday morning in the middle of May to tell the staff that he had arranged for the office to be redecorated, he was greeted with uproar.

In planning changes, people's reactions should be anticipated so you can allow the time and energy needed to deal with them. A positive response to their concerns will encourage your staff to express them fully. But people do not come out with their fears or worries just because you say you have an open door policy. They may be embarrassed or too ashamed to ask the questions they need answered. They will not want to be seen as being against you and your plans. They will not want to look foolish in front of their colleagues, some of whom will be raring to go. Instead they are likely to sit quietly hoping that things will become clearer as time goes by. If the mists do not roll back, the individual will be left with a tangle of worries which will inhibit their thinking and slow down their ability to learn the new ways of working.

There are occasions when it is better to allow certain changes to lie until the conditions are more conducive to implementing them. In the above example, some of the changes were being imposed from outside and obviously needed to be dealt with, others were generated within the department and would have little impact on improving the quality of the service offered to customers and the level of business activity. However, by implementing them at the same time as the other changes, it is possible that the staff would be overloaded and their morale and confidence levels influenced. There would be a good chance that the quality of the service offered to customers would be adversely affected. Decorating the office and introducing a new database could wait for more opportune times.

6.3 LETTING GO OF THE PAST

When new routines replace well-known ones, it is normal to experience a sense of loss. Even when the old routine was thought boring and tedious, changing it can cause an individual some difficulty. Because, in becoming unconsciously competent, we have internalised the routines and tend to revert unthinkingly to old patterns of behaviour, especially in the early stages of learning new ones. The brain has a habit of going on to automatic pilot – when we are doing one thing and thinking about another totally unrelated matter. We often slip into this mode of thinking when we are driving.

For example, imagine you have recently moved house. The route to your new home from work takes you along the same road for a while. To get to your new house you need to turn off at a junction before the one you took previously. It is very easy to come out of work, with your mind still filled with the business of the day, you get in the car and suddenly find yourself turning into the drive of your old house, with no idea of how you got there.

This same phenomenon can occur during the working day. Something takes your eye off the ball and you find yourself reverting to an old way of working, giving an outdated response or expressing a set of ideas that are not appropriate for the current conditions. In addition to preoccupation, stress and overwork often cause people to slip back into the routines and modes of thinking they know best. They are not necessarily rejecting the new ways, rather, they have not yet been able to learn them well enough. We will discuss how new routines can be learnt in ways that help them to stay firmly below.

As a manager of other people's performance, however, you need to appreciate the difficulty some people have in letting go. The stages of grieving are well known amongst bereavement counsellors and their recognition can be used to help people pass through the process. Describing the change of a work routine in the same terms as a loss that engenders feelings of grief may seem a bit extreme and over-emotional, but if the change involves separating individuals who have had a long-standing and close work relationship you are in effect, bereaving them of their friendship. And if you consider the amount of time people spend with their colleagues at work, you can see how it is possible to develop strong emotional ties.

The stages of grieving include the following symptoms.

1. **Numbness.** I don't know what, if anything, I think about it.
2. **Denial.** It can't be happening to me. This is not real.
3. **Anger.** Why me? What have I done wrong?
4. **Depression.** I don't care what happens, do what you want.
5. **Expressions of emotion.** Often crying but occasionally outbursts of temper and agitation.
6. **Insomnia and/or increased dreaming.**
7. **Lack of attention leading to poor quality work, mistakes and accidents.**
8. **Excessive enthusiasm and interests or increased levels of activity can be displayed.**
9. **Abuse of substances such as coffee, alcohol, drugs or food.**
10. **Real and psychosomatic illnesses such as stomach upsets, headaches and palpitations.**

6.4 ENDING RELATIONSHIPS

It may not seem obvious at first that you, as the manager, have a responsibility for helping your staff come to terms with the way in which organisational change may disrupt relationships. However, if you do think about what may happen and discuss the matter with the people concerned, you will find that the processes of implementing the change goes more smoothly. People, yourself included, will be better prepared for their own reaction and those of others affected by the plans.

Those affected may not just be staff employed in the section concerned. We have already discussed the identity of key players and stakeholders. In addition to the relationships formed between staff employed in the area undergoing change, we have recognised the ties customers, suppliers and colleagues can form with the people with whom they relate regularly.

Take the following scenario as an example of how to people can be prepared for change and the termination of a working relationship. Philippa is a member of a virtual organisation. She works from home 200 miles from the organisation's head office. This is staffed by a small team of five. There are twenty others in positions similar to Philippa's. They all meet twice a year and only contact each other if there is a specific need. The organisation is held together by the staff in the head office – they are the hub of the wheel. One member of staff, Peter, is the main contact point for all the members of the organisation. He manages their workload and often is in daily contact with them. Peter and Philippa have hit it off very well, despite the fact that they have met only once for about ten minutes. Over the years, they have developed a close relationship which has extended from work to personal matters and they provide good support for each other.

The organisation's chief executive decides that the head office needs refreshing. The five staff have been in their existing roles for long periods of time. He feels that they are getting stale and complacent and would benefit from a spring clean. The need for new computer hardware provides the impetus. The new system will include electronic mail. Changes to the staff's roles and new ways of working will complement the new system.

There are two ways in which the process can be managed:

1. The chief executive defines the new roles, decides who will be doing what and tells the staff accordingly. The new computers are delivered the same day and people are asked to get on with learning how to use the new software. The organisation's members find out what is happening when they next ring in.

2. The chief executive warns all the associates and staff that new systems are to be introduced the following month. Staff are asked to start thinking about how the new computers will affect their work and who should be doing what in future. The associates are warned that staff's roles may change. They are all encouraged to discuss the implications and highlight any areas that may have a negative effect on their working arrangements.

The consequences of (1) are that Peter is moved into a role that denies him contact with the associates. He misses the relationships he has spent time and effort building up and struggles to learn the new computer system. It doesn't make sense to him. He finds his new role stressful and ceases to enjoy his job. Philippa, one of the hardest working associates, is offended and hurt. She decides that if that is the way the chief executive treats people she does not want to associate herself with the organisation in future. She starts to find new outlets for her talents.

The consequences of (2) are that Peter is involved in developing the new system and is able to tell the chief executive how important regular contact with the office is for the associates, in particular how it helps Philippa to feel involved as she tends to feel a little isolated. He also tells the CE how much he enjoys the networking aspect of his work.

The chief executive is able to reflect on this and so can discuss the importance of networking with all the associates. Together, they consider how relationships with all the staff and themselves can be improved as a result of the new e-mail facility. They decide to set up an e-mail box and a bulletin board. This will be among

Peter's new responsibilities. A weekly 'gossip' sheet will be sent out so that everyone knows what is going on between the hub and the rim of the organisation. Associates and staff will be free to join in or not as they wish.

Phillipa thinks the new idea is brilliant. She is flattered as a result of being asked to contribute to the development of new ways of working. She is looking forward to getting to know the other staff in the head office better and is happy that she and Peter will be able to remain in close contact – through e-mail rather than the telephone line.

Which is the most effective way of managing change and the one most likely to have long-lasting positive results?

On a sad and final point – how often we do recognise the consequences of a terminal break in a working relationship? Staff leave for all sorts of reasons and cease to have contact with their colleagues, also, sadly, staff die. Sometimes this is sudden, sometimes after illness. It is a natural part of life and is likely to happen more often as the working population ages.

Increasing numbers of organisations are recognising that staff have responsibilities for the care of others in addition to children. Spouses and parents fall ill and need looking after. Some of the more enlightened organisations have introduced family friendly policies and the right for time off is provided for in the EU Social Charter. Some employers provide employee assistance units to help staff cope with stress and emotional reactions regardless of the cause. Many allow time off work for compassionate reasons, including the death of family members. Most managers recognise that staff's performance is likely to be adversely affected following bereavement. Allowances are made in their workload and acknowledgement given to their need for emotional support. However, few organisations extend these provisions to staff following the death of a colleague.

6.5 LEARNING NEW ROUTINES

Helping people to adopt new routines and ways of working is a critical role for any manager – if only to ensure that they are learnt properly. How quickly they can be put into practice, effectively, will directly affect the success of any new venture. This means that the old ways and previous patterns of thinking need to be:

(a) **unfrozen**: people become aware of what they are doing, what their belief systems are and the origin of those beliefs;

(b) **changed**: people learn new ideas and ways of working easily, quickly and effectively. This stage includes reminding people of the skills of learning. There is no point in replacing one set of behaviours with another that are as rigid and difficult to change as the first set;

(c) **refrozen**: the new ways become part of the individual's everyday behaviour and thinking patterns and learning how to learn is normal.

Introducing Change

Warn people that things are to happen but try to avoid frightening or threatening them. Prepare the ground and make as much as possible certain. The reason that many managers are reluctant to tell staff about change in the early planning stages is because they:

(a) fear adverse reactions especially if they are unable to tell staff the whole picture;

(b) don't want to appear incompetent because they are, at that stage, unable to answer every question;

(c) don't want staff to get the wrong end of the stick and form the wrong impression;

(d) give advance information to opponents and competitors;

(e) don't want to give enemies the time to harness their resources to oppose the final plan.

All of these reasons portray the staff in a very poor light. They are cast as the enemy or as being incapable of dealing with uncertainty. This attitude is hardly designed to encourage staff to support their manager and approach the plans for change in a positive fashion. It does not say to staff that they are members of the team with a valid contribution to make and are respected as adults.

Obviously when and how much information can be given to staff is a matter of choice and we discussed above some of the issues that need to be considered when you decide what to tell to whom, when and how. Generally speaking, if staff are informed early about change, they respect the confidence their managers place in them and respond accordingly. If they are taken into partnership, they will act as responsible partners. The chances of this are increased when the manager acknowledges their reactions, whatever they may be, as legitimate and is prepared to deal with any concerns the staff may have.

When faced with the prospect of things changing, people are unsettled by what they do not know more than by what they do know. Their first question usually is: 'What does this mean to me?' If you can answer in a confident and convincing manner, you will reassure them and are well on the way to gaining acceptance of the plan. Of course, you should not lie or make things up. If you do, you will surely be found out in time.

You can help people deal with uncertainty by dividing the future into quadrants as in Figure 6.5.

Figure 6.5: The future in quadrants

What is known now	What will be known soon
The factual information. If some of it has commercial or other sensitivities, tell the staff what these are and explain why certain parts of the plan need to remain confidential. If other matters can be open to public discussion, make this clear too.	Even if you do not know the content of future decisions you will know their scope, when they are likely to be made, who will be involved in making them and when you should be able to tell the staff about this part of the plan.
What is still to be decided	**What you don't know about**
If you are able to define the area of the unknown you will help people to put the zones of uncertainty into the context of the whole. They may not know the answers but at least they will know what is being done to answer the questions. They may also raise aspects of the plan that you have not thought about and so alert you to potential problems or weaknesses.	These are the weak aspects of your plan. You can not prepare for the totally unknown and unlikely. But by involving your staff, you increase the available experience and knowledge. You also increase the size of the network and improve the intelligence at your disposal.

Identify what Staff will need to Learn

Once the plan has some boundaries and all possible areas of uncertainty are dealt with, you and your team will be ready to start deciding who will be doing what and defining the tasks to be done to achieve the objectives. This definition will help identify who will need to learn what to perform the new tasks. The following steps will help to determine learning needs.

1. Identify components of the new roles.

2. Separate the distinct aspects of the new tasks.

3. Analyse those tasks in terms of the skills, knowledge and abilities required to perform them effectively.

4. Compare staff's current levels of knowledge, skills and abilities with those required to complete the new tasks.

5. Devise appropriate ways of enabling staff, individually or as a group, to acquire those skills, abilities and knowledge currently not present, and of enhancing those in need of improvement.

6. Make sure that the required action is taken to help the staff learn what is needed.

Learning Curve

Learning anything new takes time and the brain needs to have space to accommodate the new skills and knowledge. People do not learn well if they are overworked, under pressure, afraid and not able to concentrate. Managers are responsible for ensuring that a climate conducive to learning is created. 'We are a learning company' can be a bland statement often thrown out almost as a platitude, or as the latest fashion statement in management philosophy. If the plans are to be successful and the wellbeing of staff preserved, everyone, managers and staff alike, needs to be helped to embrace the new ways of working positively and quickly. If they do not, the chances of failure are increased and the manager will (and should) be held to account.

When we talk of learning needs we tend to assume that we are starting with a blank sheet of paper. This is not the case with adults. They come with experience, abilities, and as we discussed earlier, attitudes. The learning curve is often portrayed as in Figure 6.6.

Figure 6.6: The learning curve as portrayed

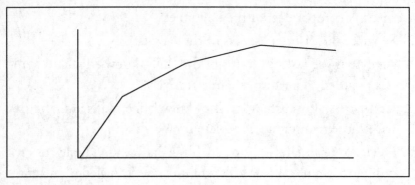

Actually Figure 6.6 misrepresents the truth. A more realistic diagram is shown in Figure 6.7.

Figure 6.7: The real learning curve

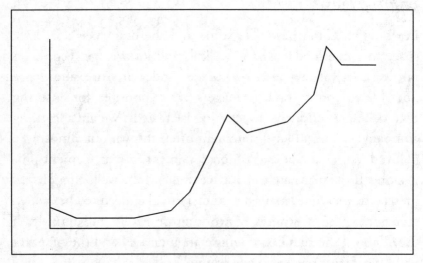

Initially, as people realise their lack of knowledge and their self-confidence suffers, their competency drops. Their learning is incremental and sometimes it may stop or even drop back.

Learning is an ongoing process, building on what is already known and developing existing skills. One of the biggest challenges for those assisting the learning of others is helping them unlearn well-known routines and habits. There is a danger of seeing all previous learning as being outdated. This is not the case. It provides the platform from which to build and develop. Past experiences are the beginnings of wisdom and sometimes old ways can again offer solutions to new problems.

Kolb[2] identified a cycle containing four stages, each of which need to be passed through for effective learning to take place. Effective learning is that which results in enduring change. Learning is not just education and training. It is more than experience. It is the process that takes place within the individual. It is not external; although external events can stimulate learning. Learning happens within the individual and effective learning results in enduring change (see Figure 6.8).

Figure 6.8: The Kolb cycle

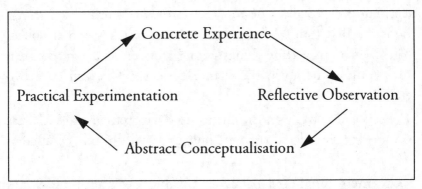

Actual experience needs to be followed by a period of reflection. This can include discussing the experience with colleagues and considering its meaning. Forming more widely applicable concepts usually results from the mental processes that follow reflection. During these, the new ideas are compared and melded with those previously learnt. New concepts are formed and stored in the memory. These are then tried out and the associated skills practised. Feedback may be obtained as a result of trials and fur-

2. Kolb, *Experiential Learning: Experiences as the Sources of Learning and Development* (1984).

ther reflection takes place as more experience is gained. Thus the cycle is completed and forms part of the upward spiral of growth and development.

The manager's role is to provide the support needed for each stage of learning to be completed fully and is consolidated. Practical support comes from opportunities for practice and the provision of good quality information about performance. This information should be focused and detailed. Even when you give praise, the member of staff needs to know what they did right so it can be repeated. This is just as important as information about behaviour that was not up to the standard required.

Making Mistakes

The opportunity to make mistakes is an important part of the learning cycle. Sadly, due to the pressures at work to get things right the first time, the value of making mistakes is overlooked. The chances of getting things wrong are seen as being too great for people to be given the chance to learn. This can have two effects:

1. People are not given the chance to develop their skills as areas of work considered risky are only allocated to fully competent staff.

2. Learners can be so paralysed by the fear of getting things wrong that they do not take the risks and so are not able to complete the learning cycle.

As the manager, it is up to you to create the sort of situation where people are able to try out newly acquired skills and knowledge. If this means devising simulations or having dry runs to reduce the level of risk, so be it. If dry runs are not possible, you may find it necessary to supervise their work in the early stages. The word has attracted some poor connotations as it is taken to imply overseeing, controlling and interfering. But supervision can also mean quiet observation and the provision of feedback.

Alternatively, you may find it useful to hold briefing sessions and help an individual check their preparation before entering into a real life situation. You may also wish to organise post-experience reviews to go through what happened and ensure that the reflection stage takes place. Over the long-term, you will be able to help the individual compare their separate experiences and draw out the generally applicable concepts.

The importance of good quality feedback cannot be over-stressed. Without detailed information it is not possible for the learner to know what worked and where improvement is required. For some reason, many managers find giving feedback difficult. Some do not like praising people – they might get big headed and have ideas above their station. Equally, they do not like giving criticism – it may cause offence or upset the person. Neither of these are good reasons for not providing factual information about the results of an individual's behaviour at work.

A checklist to help you provide good quality feedback without falling into the trap of being negative and destructive or excessively complimentary was given in Chapter 3.

6.6 GETTING TO KNOW NEW PEOPLE

How well new people are brought into the existing team can have a direct effect on their abilities to do their job in the long-term. The first day tends to pass in a whizz of information, hellos and unremembered details. The period following the first day makes the difference. This is when the individual begins to understand the expectations of the organisation, your requirements and finds out whether their own ambitions will be realised. This period can be divided into three stages that usually run parallel with each other.

Induction

This stage is when the information the individual needs about the organisation and the job is transmitted. Some organisations make use of checklists and manuals to ensure that all the necessary information is supplied, accurately. The sort of information included can range from an outline of the organisation's mission and purpose to seemingly minor details, such as where to get stationery.

Often the minor details can make the difference. While the big picture information puts the job into its broader context and enables the individual to locate themselves in relation to the aims and the work of colleagues, the detail can have a direct bearing on performance.

If you decide a checklist would be useful, you might find talking to some recent new starters illuminating. Ask them what was essential, desirable and nice to know in their first day, week and month. What was omitted and what irrelevant information was given to them.

Inclusion

The second stage is the one in which the new starter is accepted or rejected by the existing work team. Obviously, if the team finds it impossible to include the new starter in membership, the new person will find it exceedingly difficult to succeed in their job.

Teams have formal systems and relationships. These are the ones set down by the organisation. The leader is named and work allocated according to job descriptions and priorities. There are other less formal systems and structures which lie beneath the surface. These dynamics make the team work or not. Alongside the formal leader, often a social leader can be found. The formal leader may have the authority gained from status, the informal leader is the one who exercises influence and power over the other members.

We discussed in Chapter 2 the processes used to set standards and outlined the ways in which those used by the team can be different to those set by the manager. We also discussed how ways of working can be approved by the team or found to be unacceptable. These levels can result in high performance or enable the members to get away with the minimum.

Groups can be quite ferocious in the way in which they treat new members who do not fit in or are unable to comply with the norms of behaviour and value systems. The new person is subjected to peer pressure which 'encourages' them to comply. We referred above to the effects found during the Hawthorne Experiments and how individuals are drawn into the circle.

The opposite can also be seen. The individual is regarded as an outsider if they are not prepared to join in. They are denied information they need to do their job. Gradually, fewer and fewer people talk to them and finally they suffer the organisational equivalent of being sent to Coventry. You need to be aware of the dynamics of the group. You may not be able to intervene directly, but you need to be sure that they are not getting in the way of the new member of staff doing their job.

Ideas such as buddying – when an existing member of staff (possibly the social leader or a close colleague of that person) is asked to take the new starter under their wing – can result in the fast inclusion of new starters and thus reduce the time needed for them to become fully effective.

Buddying schemes are most often used for junior staff. Some similar schemes exist for managers. These are generally called mentoring and were discussed earlier. Regardless of the name, the importance is the recognition of the underlying processes and the need for a new starter to learn how to become a member of the work group.

Initial Learning

The third stage is when the individual learns how to do the job. Even when the new starter is highly experienced, much of that experience will have been gained in other organisations. They will need to learn your systems and procedures and, especially, your ways of doing things. No matter how skilled the new starter may be, their abilities will have been developed in the context of their previous employer. They will need to adapt to your systems and, as we have discussed above, learn how to work with their new colleagues.

If your recruitment and selection process has been thorough, an assessment of competency will have been conducted. This will have highlighted strengths and provided the reasons for the chosen individual's appointment. It will also have indicated areas where improvements could be made. These are seldom recognised at the time of appointment. There is an assumption that the successful candidate, being the best, is in fact a perfect match with the criteria. In reality this situation rarely occurs. More often, the individual has some shortcomings, many of which can easily be overcome. The assessment can therefore provide the foundation for the creation of an initial training plan.

You will need to spend time with the new starter going through working methods and checking their assumptions. If this is not done, it is possible that the individual will walk, unprepared, into a minefield.

Take Martin, for example. He was an experienced surveyor well used to managing his own clients. His previous employer was in the habit of submitting accounts to clients at the end of the project or as agreed in the terms of contract. His new employer, a larger company, billed its clients monthly. Each fee earner was expected to submit a monthly timesheet to the finance department showing how long had been spent on each account. In addition, it was expected that a project report be appended which indicated, for each client, progress against target and an assessment of future earnings potential. Each report was to be signed off by a managing partner who was expected to make comments.

No one had told Martin about this system. Four months into his appointment, he was shocked to be called to the Finance Director to explain why he had not earned anything since he was appointed. It took quite a long time for Martin and the Finance Director to realise what had happened. Even when the system had been explained, Martin remained shocked by the way he had been treated and was appalled by the high level of control exercised by the company over its professional staff. He began to question whether his decision to join the company had been wise.

Simple misunderstandings during the initial phase can be disastrous on a number of levels. The individual may find that:

(a) the lack of early information about the employer leads to unacceptably high levels of confusion;

(b) their new colleagues are unfriendly and difficult to work with;

(c) the lack of initial training and support means they are not able to meet the standards;

(d) they fail to achieve the levels of potential predicted during the selection process and end up disappointing themselves and you, their new manager.

This is not a happy set of scenarios but they can all be avoided if the induction period is approached systematically.

6.7 SUMMARY

In this chapter we have looked at the consequences of letting go old ways and routines of working. These may be boring and even hated, but they form part of an individual's being. If the routines have been followed for long periods, expecting a member of staff simply to stop doing a task one way and start doing it another, may be asking too much. Learning new ways of working takes time. Unlearning the old ways can require similar levels of support and tolerance. Sadly, often when engaging in organisational change we do not give adequate recognition to this. Nor do we acknowledge that emotions may be involved.

These emotions may be hidden but they may nevertheless exist. And they may be unexpectedly profound. The individual may display reactions that can appear to be over the top or inappropriate. This could be simply because they are experiencing a reaction similar to that displayed after a bereavement.

It is possible to consider the likely reactions of staff when planning change. If these are anticipated, it is possible to build in allowances and time for staff to ensure they fully understand the implications of the changes for their daily routines and relationships. It also allows time for them to learn the new ways of working properly and consolidate them into everyday practices.

Managers are not excluded from these reactions and the need for time and space to learn. If some of the ideas we have been discussing here are new to you, you will need time and brain space to consider them and reflect on how you may make use of them in your work. You will want to compare them with other experiences and ideas you have encountered and possibly try out one or two ideas. The next chapter is devoted to looking at how you might do this.

PUTTING NEW WAYS OF MANAGING INTO PRACTICE

7.1 INTRODUCTION

In this final chapter we will look at how to put the ideas outlined previously into practice. Before you start putting new ways of managing into practice, you may wish to consider your existing skill levels. You may be extremely competent across the board, but it is possible that some aspects of your performance could be improved. It is also possible that some of the ideas discussed already are totally new, requiring you to learn a fresh set of skills. All the comments made earlier about the individual needing support and feedback apply to you just as much as they do to your staff.

During learning, you may experience the same feelings of fear and uncertainty and may find questioning your existing underpinning values and belief systems is an uncomfortable process. However, just as you have been urged to be patient and fair to your staff, you should be fair to yourself. Developing new skills is not something that happens overnight. Learning takes time. It also needs to be supported.

This chapter is intended to provide some of that support. It will suggest some areas you may need to address and will offer ideas on how you might deal with the issues encountered. You are likely to face the same challenges as anyone developing their skills, but as a manager, you may find that you have to deal some further factors. In addition to your own expectations you will have to satisfy those of your manager and colleagues. You will also find that your staff have views and expectations about your behaviour. You may find that all of these place constraints on your ability to develop your own style. However, rather than treating them as rigid boundaries, you should regard them simply as other parts of the process to be dealt with.

We will start with an instrument designed to help you explore your perceptions of others and yourself. This is intended to help you question your assumptions as a manager and then consider whether they are still appropriate. You will be encouraged to identify which, if any, need to be reassessed for your current context and the future. We will then look at the factors that influence your leadership style.

7.2 HOW YOU SEE YOURSELF AND OTHERS

The questionnaire in Figure 7.1 has been designed to help you think about how you manage your staff. Please remember at the outset that there are no rights and wrongs. We all develop our own style from our previous experiences and our beliefs. We also tend to copy the behaviour of other people – sometimes unconsciously. These and other factors combine to influence the way we treat other people. Sometimes this will be appropriate and lead to productive working relationships. At other times relationships will be not so good and may have been produced as a result of your reaction to a particular situation.

Different factors come into play, many of which are outside the control of the manager, but how each manager behaves towards their staff is within the control of the individual. We all have some choice in our reactions and, as discussed above, we are able to change our attitudes if the need is great enough. The questionnaire has been designed to help you consider if there is anything in your present frame of reference that you would like to change.

Figure 7.1: Questionnaire to determine what you need to change

Scoring: 1 = I do this most often; 2 = I do this on occasion; 3 = I sometimes do this; 4 = I do this infrequently; 5 = I rarely do this. Enter your scores in the appropriate boxes in Figure 7.2 and then add up the scores for each column.

	1	2	3	4	5
1. I need to monitor my staff's performance closely to ensure they work as well as they are able.					
2. I encourage team members to make important decisions and involve them in setting objectives.					
3. I establish the goals and standards for the team to achieve.					
4. I appraise individual's performance regularly against their agreed targets and encourage them to think ahead about their future development needs.					
5. I need to watch my staff's progress carefully and take early action if I think things are going awry.					
6. I hold regular meetings so that team members can bring me up to date with our progress in achieving our objectives and let me know if there are any areas of concern.					
7. I plan the team's work carefully to make sure that no one person is overloaded.					
8. The team reviews its priorities and agrees any alteration with me.					

	1	2	3	4	5
9. I welcome new ideas from the team and am pleased when they solve their own problems.					
10.I am available if anyone wishes to discuss a work-related or other matter with me.					
11.I need to take most of the decisions as members of the team are not very interested in their work.					
12.As the team is reluctant to take on new areas of work, I have to give them clear instructions outlining what has to be done when.					
13.I encourage members of the team to take responsibility for their own work so they do not need detailed instructions.					
14.I find that I need to keep on top of staff to ensure that deadlines are met.					

Figure 7.2: Scoring for questionnaire

Column A	
1	
3	
5	
7	
11	
12	
14	
Total	

Column B	
2	
4	
6	
8	
9	
10	
13	
Total	

Plot on the scale in figure 7.3 where your scores for each column lie.

Figure 7.3: Douglas McGregor's theories

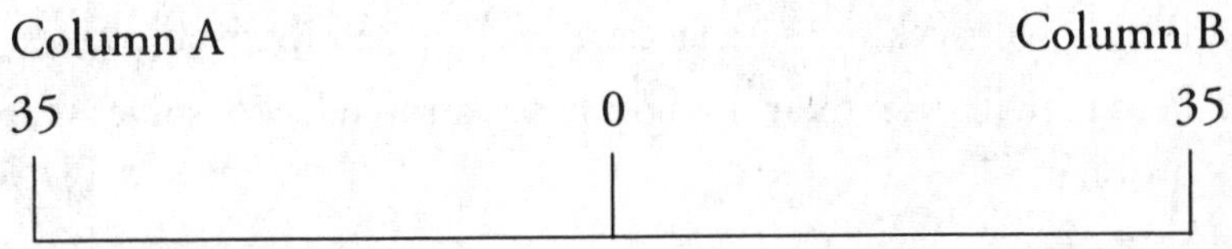

Column A   Column B

35   0   35

Note: Column A represents a view of people which Douglas McGregor called *Theory X*. Column B represents his *Theory* Y.[1] The Lower your score in Column A the closer you are to Theory X. The higher your score in Column B the closer you are to Theory Y.

Theory X Assumptions

1. People, in general, dislike work and will avoid it if possible.
2. People need to be given precise directions.
3. People try to avoid responsibility.
4. People need to be threatened with punishment or the withholding of rewards if they are to work to the required standards.
5. People need to be coerced and controlled to make sure they work to the required standards.
6. People generally seek security and are not ambitious.

Theory Y Assumptions

1. People enjoy working as it is as natural as rest and play.
2. People are able to direct their own efforts to attaining the objectives they are committed to.

---

1. McGregor, *The Human Side of Enterprise* (1960).

3. People are able to exercise self-control and will accept responsibility for their own work.

4. People will set their own standards and monitor their performance against their objectives.

5. People will seek the satisfaction of attaining their objectives.

6. People will use their imagination and help to solve shared problems.

This theory was developed some time ago and is seen by some as a simplified polarisation of people's belief systems. Nevertheless, it serves to show how the manager's view of staff affects the way they are managed and treated. How staff are treated affects the way they respond.

It would be wrong to imply that there is one right style of managing staff. As we will see below there are many other factors, in addition to personal beliefs that affect a manager's style. These do not necessarily constrain your behaviour. Nor do they deny you the opportunity to change it if you think you could do better. But before making any changes, you should ask yourself the following questions.

1. Are my beliefs and behaviour appropriate for my current work team and situation?

2. Which aspects, if any, need to be altered to make them more appropriate for the current or future situation?

7.3   LEADERSHIP STYLE

The debate about whether leaders are born or made has raged for-ever, and continues so to do. At first, it was believed that leaders were given their authority, often as a result of their parentage. Some claimed their right was God-given. Many of these people had to work hard to retain their position or face the real possibil-ity of being overthrown. Later leaders gained their position by using their skills to command resources and people. These skills included the abilities to influence and inspire others, select loyal lieutenants and deal effectively with opponents.

Interest in defining the skills of leadership has run alongside the wish to understand the factors that drive personal relation-ships and group dynamics. The search for greater insight into the management process has also led to the attempts to differentiate between a manager and a leader. Many years of research and large sums of money have been devoted to this search. The total amount of time given to debating the topics must extend into centuries. Still there is no conclusive answer. If anything, the question has grown bigger and more complex. We are concerned not only with whether or not a good leader is a product of breed-ing or learning, but also to know if different cultures contain their own unique approaches. Do men and women have different leadership qualities? If the very best leaders are born skilled, is it possible for others to develop those skills?

The safest course of action is to leave the debate for another time. Instead we will concentrate here on the other factors which, regardless of skills and style, affect leadership and its effectiveness.

Figure 7.4: Factors affecting leadership style

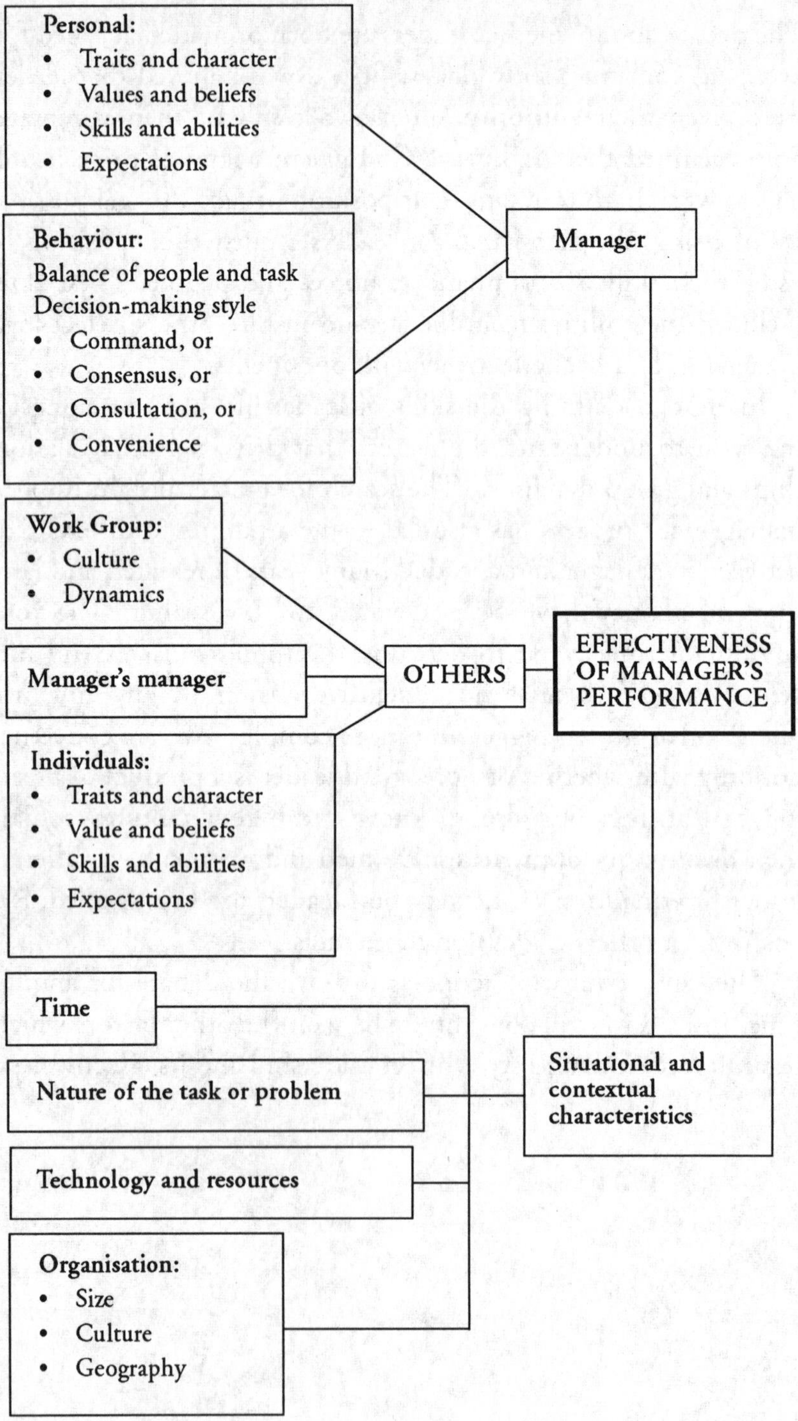

Personal:
- Traits and character
- Values and beliefs
- Skills and abilities
- Expectations

Behaviour:
Balance of people and task
Decision-making style
- Command, or
- Consensus, or
- Consultation, or
- Convenience

Manager

Work Group:
- Culture
- Dynamics

Manager's manager

OTHERS

EFFECTIVENESS OF MANAGER'S PERFORMANCE

Individuals:
- Traits and character
- Value and beliefs
- Skills and abilities
- Expectations

Time

Nature of the task or problem

Technology and resources

Organisation:
- Size
- Culture
- Geography

Situational and contextual characteristics

Can you add any other factors that affect your situation and limit your scope for action? Once you have identified the forces that are pressing on you, you are in a position to decide which you want to alter so that have you will have greater freedom in your leadership style.

Many managers feel unable to change the way they manage. They believe that the factors surrounding them are fixed. They think they have little scope for manoeuvre. They see themselves as being confined by organisational walls and hemmed in by others' expectations. Sometimes this is true, but often they have more scope for action than they think. The walls may be further away or they may be built of paper rather than brick. Until it is tested, the reality will not be known.

Do you know which of your limits are rigid and unmoveable and which can be changed? Once you know where you stand, you are better able to decide which aspects of your behaviour you want to change. You may find it helpful to work with a colleague, or perhaps a small group of colleagues, who also want to develop their skills. You will thus be able to assist each other's learning by:

(a) providing support;

(b) listening;

(c) asking each other searching questions;

(d) helping the others to reflect and think hard;

(e) contributing from your experience and ideas;

(f) giving each other good quality feedback.

Groups such as these are sometimes called Action Learning Sets. They do not need permission to be set up and do not require resources, but they do need the following.

1. **Loyalty and commitment.** If people do not attend regularly, learning sets do not function.

2. **Agreement to confidentiality.** People are not going to share their learning needs and especially their fears if they are unable to trust the other members.

3. The creation of a climate where the participants are able to be open with each other and themselves.

4. Open-mindedness and commitment to learning.

7.4   MAKING CHANGES

Step One

The first step is the identification of what you need to learn. This is far easier said than done, especially in people management where interpersonal skills have a major role to play. They tend to be described in intangible terms so it is important to break down the general into specific parts, then you can identify which aspects need to be changed.

You may be experiencing a sense of discontent or dissatisfaction with your own performance. It is possible that you do not know exactly where the source of this feeling lies. You may have a feeling of things not being right but do not know how to make things better. Obviously, you will need to narrow the range of options. You can not improve on everything at once. You need to know where to start and which aspects of your performance need the most immediate action.

If you consider those areas that you know are going well, you will be able to rule out aspects of your performance that do not need immediate attention. If you think hard enough you will know which these are. You could well have some external evidence to back up your opinion. You may find it useful to note down your own appraisal in a grid such as Figure 7.5.

Figure 7.5: Positive self-appraisal grid

Aspect of performance	Reasons for believing it is working well	Evidence to support belief
Running staff meetings.	We get the business completed quickly and make decisions.	Action is taken as a result of the decisions. Staff say the meetings work.
Delegating.	Staff do not come back with questions after being given a task.	Very few mistakes are made. Most tasks are completed to the standard expected.

Then you need to think about those areas of your work that are not going so well. A similar grid may again be helpful (see Figure 7.6).

Figure 7.6: Negative self-appraisal grid

Aspect of performance	Reasons for believing it is not working well	Evidence to support belief
Forward planning.	We tend to deal with just today's needs and do not discuss what might happen next week, never mind next month.	We are often taken by surprise. We are unprepared for things that could easily have been predicted.
Lack of clear goals.	Our portfolio of activities is a mess. Operations are competing for resources. No one knows who is doing what or why.	There is no underpinning rationale to explain our actions. We take on every opportunity whether it fits with other activities or not.

You should also try to think about any aspects of management you are not doing. This is hard to think about on your own. For if you are not doing it, it is possible that you do not know that it should be done at all. Talking to other people about their approach and managing people in general can be most helpful.

You may be fortunate enough to receive some good quality feedback from a colleague or a member of your team. Receiving feedback from your staff is a privilege. Not many people feel able to talk frankly to their boss about how they think they are being managed and led. No matter how flat the structure, how open the culture and how balanced the psychological contract may be, there will always be a power dimension to the relationship that makes it difficult to be honest with the boss. If your staff are able to give you feedback, you should think for a few seconds about your ability to do the same for your boss, before doing anything at all.

Receiving feedback is never easy. It can be even more difficult when it comes from the people who report to you. A natural, immediate response is to justify your behaviour and defend your actions. But before responding, remember that at the very least, your staff deserve to be heard, if for no other reason than to recognise their courage to talk to you in such a way. At the very best, they will be giving you the very information you need to improve your performance.

Some organisations have instituted 360° appraisal schemes to aid the exchange of information between managers, their manager, their staff and colleagues. Some companies also include customers. The purpose of such schemes is twofold. Firstly, they exist formally to make sure the exchange happens. Secondly, they provide the means of making the feedback anonymous believing this will enable people to be more honest.

If you feel that you have not yet created relationships that are strong enough to allow an open, unstructured exchange of information, you may find some of the listings of management behaviour and activities helpful, such as the Occupational Standards published by the Management Charter Initiative. These are used to assess achievement for the National Vocational Qualification and are available at levels 3, 4 and 5. They tend to focus on the outcomes of performance in a range of activities and seek evidence of underpinning knowledge.

Other lists of management behaviour are more behaviourally focused, such as the criteria used for the assessment of abilities in assessment and development centres. Some of the big publishers of psychometric tests, such as Saville and Holdsworth and DDI, have their own competency statements and some organisations, particularly the very large employers, develop their own standards and sought behaviour. Other sources include books and articles on the topic of management behaviour. These range in seriousness. Some are a bit like magazine quizzes. Others are sophisticated and well-tested instruments designed to help managers engage in self-development. Perhaps the most useful and long lasting is *A Manager's Guide to Self-development* by Pedler, Burgoyne and Boydell.[2]

Such lists are useful as benchmarks to help you compare yourself with external models and standards. Their downside is that they are generalisations and do not take account of your situation and the people surrounding you. Even so, they will help you to focus on specific areas and support your own analysis of your strengths and weaknesses.

Step Two

Once you have identified the particular aspects of your behaviour you want to work on, you need to start thinking about how to develop those skills and make changes to your behaviour. Before we consider this, the following should be stressed.

1. Everyone is a mixture of strengths and weaknesses. No one is perfect.
2. In the current situation, previous strengths may be weaknesses.

---

2. Pedler, Burgoyne & Boydell, *A Manager's Guide to Self Development* (1994).

3. A strength in excess can be a weakness.

4. If strengths are not maintained, they fall into disuse and can become weaknesses.

The last point in particular is worth remembering. If you concentrate just on getting the weaknesses up to scratch and neglect your strengths, you may find that you are creating unnecessary problems for the future.

Having identified the priority areas, you may wish to consider their comparative importance in relation to action needed to maintain your strengths, the demands of your daily work and the rest of your life. It is easy, when thinking about negatives, to get them out of proportion. This can be as dangerous as doing nothing. If you rush about trying to improve on all fronts, there is a chance of making matters worse for yourself and the other people you work with. Instead, for a little while:

(a)   stand back;

(b)   reflect;

(c)   prioritise;

(d)   plan; and then

(e)   act.

Figure 7.7 may be a useful example. Compiling your own list may help you place, in order of importance, the aspects of your behaviour that need your conscious attention. It may also help you think about the best form of action to take.

Figure 7.7: Aspects of your behaviour that may need attention

	Comments	Critical to long-term success	Urgent attention is needed to deal with particular situations	Important but can wait	Desirable
Weaknesses					
Improve delegation skills.	Staff coming back with too many questions and complaining about being confused.		Yes		
Increase ability to forecast.	Too many problems take me by surprise.	Yes			
Strengths					
Openness with staff.	Danger of letting other tasks stop me talking to staff.	Yes			
Technical knowledge.	Need to keep up to date.			Yes	

	Comments	Critical to long-term success	Urgent attention is needed to deal with particular situations	Important but can wait	Desirable
Tasks					
Monthly reports must be completed on time.	Need to make sure enough time is left for this.				Yes
Talk to staff about last week's complaint from customer.			Yes		
Rest of life					
Spend enjoyable time with family.	Too often spend Sunday afternoons catching up on reading and doing monthly reports.	Yes			
Learn computer skills.	Will help with scheduling and planning.		Yes		Yes

Once you know the *what* (the specific areas you need to work on) and the *whys,* you can start to consider the *hows* and the *whens*.

The Hows

There are many different ways of developing skills. Most of these are not dependent on going on a course. Pedler *et al.*[3] make some useful suggestions as do Chambers, Coopey and McLean.[4] Some development techniques which can be used alone, with others and with your staff are described by Dale.[5]

Reading about management skills, as well as giving information about the whys, whats and hows, helps to promote reflection. We are not always able to give enough time to this important activity. Reflecting is more than just thinking about past events. It can be hard work as the thoughts need to be focused on to specific aspects and result in conclusions. This is not the normal way of thinking, as the brain cannot be allowed simply to idle along. You may find that you need some way of imposing a structure or discipline on your mind.

Discussing and debating issues with helpful others can focus your attention. The purposeful discussion of an issue with another person requires it to be described. You are then able to talk around it, gaining in insight and possibly coming to a conclusion. Debating an issue means that you take a particular stance and consider in turn the pros and cons of your position. This form of structured conversation can be particularly helpful if you are not sure about the comparative merits of different courses of action. Take for example, the case of Pauline, the owner of a small business.

Her two secretaries are complaining that they are underpaid and have suggested, quite strongly that unless she does something about it they will start looking around for other jobs. Pauline knows that there is a demand for good secretarial staff in the area and hers are very experienced and competent. She also knows that she is paying them the top rate. Pauline is reluctant to pay them

---

3. Pedler *et al., op. cit.*
4. Chambers, Coopey & McLean, *Develop Your Management Potential* (1990).
5. Dale, *Developing Management Skills* (1998).

more as she thinks that would unsettle the four computer operators but she would be hard pressed to replace them if they left.

She has been thinking about the situation for the last few days
and feels caught on the horns of the proverbial dilemma:

1. Pay them more and she risks upsetting other staff.

2. Do nothing and she could lose two valuable employees.

What should she do?

Pauline decides to talk to her close friend and long-time associate, her bank manager. The manager asks Pauline one question
which threw her.

"Is there anything else going on that might have caused the
secretaries to feel undervalued?"

"I don't know," replies Pauline.

"Why not think about it and see what you can find out?"
suggests her friend.

The next day, Pauline arranges to see the secretaries and
says to them, "I know you are unhappy about your wages. Is
there anything else that is making you unhappy at work?"

The two look at each other and there is a short pause before
one says, "It's not fair. The clerks have Word 7 and we are still
on Version 2. It's not as if they do a lot of wordprocessing. We
would have put up with it if the sales staff did not tease us
every time they come into our office. We know that our computers are too old to take the new programme and you can't
afford to get us new machines, just after you have bought
those for the operators, but we feel like second class citizens
now."

"Oh dear," says Pauline. "Thank you for being honest with
me. Is there anything else at all that is making you unhappy?"

To this the second secretary says, "Well...yes. The van
driver whistles at us. We know he means no harm, but we are
fed up of being treated like floozies. We are grown women."

"Right," says Pauline. "Please leave matters with me. I will
get back to you in a couple of days."

Over the next two days Pauline kept a close watch on the secretaries' office so she could see for herself what was going on. As soon as she saw that the secretaries were not exaggerating, the sales staff and van driver were told, in no uncertain terms, that their behaviour was not acceptable. Changes were to take place immediately.

She also called her friend and having thanked him did the calculations. She worked out that increasing the secretaries' salaries by the requested £10 a week would cost more over two years than buying them new computers. The latter would have tax benefits, the former would increase her insurance contributions. Thanks to the one question from the bank manager, Pauline had escaped her dilemma.

Do you have someone outside your immediate situation to talk to? Perhaps you could find a mentor – a more experienced colleague with whom you are able to discuss matters confidentially – or maybe you have a friend who could fill this role. The friend could be someone with detailed knowledge that you can draw on or be someone who knows nothing about the detail of your situation. Sometimes a lack of detailed knowledge can be valuable. People who share your knowledge also share your assumptions and blind spots. (Remember the Johari Window?)

Action Learning Sets use this lack of detailed knowledge to good effect. Members of the set are able to ask you naïve questions, such as 'Why do you do it this way?' It is not good enough to answer 'because this is the way the organisation works'. Naïve questions are intended to make you think hard about the whys and consider if the reasons continue to be sound. If not, you have the chance of changing them. Even if you decide that change is not required, at the very least you will know why that is so. If you had not been questioned you would not know the answer. The purpose of asking naïve questions is to challenge your assumptions and force you to explore your underpinning concepts.

The first obstacle to getting help may be yourself. Asking for help may seem as though you are admitting failure or a lack of ability. There is no harm in admitting that you are not perfect. In fact, pretending you are is a bigger flaw. We all have gaps in our knowledge and skill – admitting that we need to learn and develop is a strength, not the opposite.

We are not encouraged to work collaboratively. (If you remember school, working together, unless it was on a specific team project, was frequently seen as cheating or copying.) But at work things should be different. Remember Drucker's definition of management? It suggests that a manager can only succeed if the efforts of others are focused towards the achievement of shared objectives. Some people may think that helping you may require them to give something up or weaken their position. They are wrong. If you are all working towards the organisation's objectives, collaboration not competition should be the rule.

That being said, you may still find it necessary to enter into negotiations with colleagues to gain access to the resources (including their knowledge and opinions) you need. You may even have to come to some form of deal. You may be able to offer something that will be of benefit to them. Perhaps the idea of establishing a Learning Set will also help their learning by enabling ideas to be exchanged and by providing support in the shared venture of learning.

Space and opportunities will be needed for you to find and try out new ideas and approaches. Time is perhaps a greater commodity than money. Most often the actions needed to obtain ideas and explore different concepts cost hours rather than pounds. For example, visiting another part of your organisation to talk to colleagues about how they do a similar task, will incur possibly travel costs as well as their and your time. Talking over the telephone will add a little to your phone bill and take your and the other party's time. E-mail reduces the line costs but still takes time to write and reply to the message. But the exchange of perceptions and ideas can help you solve problems that previously were intractable.

Some organisations have recognised that such exploratory visits and exchanges of experience can have wider benefits than just the development of one individual and so have taken steps to formalise and legitimise such activities. Some are using benchmarking to compare operational efficiency, cost and effectiveness. The structure focuses attention on areas that matter and the results used to highlight which aspects of the operations would benefit from change. Follow up discussions with the comparators leads to the exchange of ideas and learning about alternative ways of working. It is then possible to decide whether to adopt the different approaches or remain the same.

Another way to consider whether or not a different approach or the use of other skills would be beneficial is a 'what-if?' analysis. To carry out this analysis, each available option or pattern of behaviour is considered and the most likely outcomes predicted. You then assess the probability of each and can include the best and the worst possible outcomes. Pauline, in the above example, could have used Figure 7.8 to consider her options.

Figure 7.8: A what-if analysis

Option	Outcome	What next	Chance of occurring
Increase the secretaries' salaries.	Increased wage costs.	Secretaries happy.	50%
		Secretaries still unhappy.	50%
	Other staff find out.	They demand an equal increase.	80%
		They don't demand an equal increase.	20%
	Other staff don't find out.		10%
Don't increase the salaries.	Secretaries remain unhappy.	One or both secretaries find other jobs.	75%

Option	Outcome	What next	Chance of occurring
		Both stay and remain unhappy.	25%
Increase everyone's salaries.	Increased wage costs.	Nothing changes.	20%
		Everyone happy.	40%
Talk to the secretaries.	Find out the real source of their grievance.	It is only the money.	40%
		There is something else going on.	60%

Pauline would have been able to focus her thoughts and guide herself in the direction most likely to produce the best way forward for her and her staff, if she had followed this analysis.

Thinking purposefully about a problem and considering a new idea takes the effort needed to make the brain work and keep its attention focused. It also takes time, for, while you are reflecting, you will find it hard to do anything else that needs mental energy. Some people find that physical exercise, such as walking, running, swimming or cycling, helps to stimulate profound thoughts. (It also helps them keep fit and this is believed to reduce stress.)

However, we must compare the cost of the time needed to reflect with the cost of doing nothing. Time is usually an opportunity cost rather than the direct expenditure of money. If you were not reflecting you would probably be doing something else. What that would be is for you to answer. You are best placed to know what you do with your day. Have you ever examined what happens to your time? Time management courses often start by suggesting that you identify where those precious minutes go.

1. Which are spent productively?
2. Which are used to help you rest and restore your energy levels?
3. Which are wasted?

You are then asked to identify the time stealers – those activities that demand your attention but result in no real benefit for you or anyone else. When you are considering whether to reflect on an issue or do something else, do you ever consider which of the two will have the greatest long-term benefit for you?

There will be times when the aspects of your behaviour you want to change will require something more than just considering new ideas, alternative approaches or different people's experiences. You may need to acquire new skills. This can be done through a simulation of the situation or problem. Doing this will create a learning activity similar to the role-plays used in some training courses. These create a setting which allows the participants to experiment in safe, controlled situations. They can try out patterns of behaviour they would not risk in real life. You can create this sort of setting for yourself, but you may need help in the following areas so the situation or representation of the problem is a realistic representation of life.

1. Set up the situation or setting.
2. Take part and respond as they would in real life to your actions.
3. Engage in active reflection of the experience.
4. Provide good quality feedback.
5. Repeat the experience so that you can try different approaches or get better by practising.

Your helpful others may be prepared to let you shadow them. This is a useful way of observing more experienced people using their skills. Purposeful shadowing involves:

(a) watching them at work, paying detailed attention to what they do and say;
(b) making notes of what happens and your thoughts;

(c) observing the reactions obtained from other people;

(d) carrying out the activity, repeating what you have observed;

(e) receiving feedback from your helpful others (and possibly the other people involved);

(f) trying again;

(g) being coached by your helpful others;

(h) trying again.

The purpose of such simulations and shadowing is to allow you to experiment with different approaches and get the feel of using different skills in comparatively safe situations. Once you feel reasonably comfortable with your new approach, the time is right to put it into practice for real.

Practice

We do not give enough recognition of the need for practice in real life. When receiving medical treatment, you may find that you are asked if you mind being examined by a student. Most of us agree, because we know that if we are to have competent clinicians in the future, they need to learn on real people at some point in their training. How many of us are more tolerant of learner drivers? Do we remember that we too had to learn at sometime? Do you create safe but real learning situations for your staff? Are you prepared to give them the tolerance they deserve as learners? Do you create such a space for yourself?

If you are to develop new skills and refine them you will need to *practice, practice and practice*. Practice means giving yourself the chance to make mistakes and the opportunity to get better. If you are doing something new, it is not fair to expect yourself to be perfect the first or even the second time. Rehearsals (or simulations) can be so important if real life is too risky. There is no excuse for ignoring the following adage: Proper Preparation Prevents Poor Performance.

Feedback is an integral part of practice as is coaching. It stops you developing bad habits. It also helps to identify the aspects of your behaviour which are working well and those in need further work. Feedback also helps you assess the consequences of your behaviour. If possible, obtaining evidence in addition to feedback may be worthwhile. For example, after your first staff meeting, try asking one or two of the participants to comment on how they thought it had gone. Ask them what went well for them and what could be done better next time to improve the conduct of the meeting. There is no shame in saying that it was your first such meeting and that you want to learn from the experience. It will be easier to establish a climate in which your staff feel able to be open with you about their learning and development needs if you set the example. If the same rules for giving feedback are used by everyone, you will all learn how to focus on behaviour and avoid making personal comments more quickly.

Getting Others to Accept the New You

It is not easy for a manager to change behaviour. Others have expectations of you and may not recognise your attempts to do things differently. Their expectations, unless they also change, can trap you or force you back into previous patterns of behaviour. If we look, for example, at Steven's attempts, we can see how difficult it can be.

Steven realised, almost in a flash of the blindingly obvious, that it was possible to get people to do as he wanted without bellowing at them all the time. He had a reputation for being a hard man with high standards and was known for his habit of appearing in one of his branches unannounced. It was generally believed that he did this in the hope of catching someone out.

Steven decided to stop his spot visits and ring the staff in advance. He asked them to do nothing out of the ordinary, he just wanted to talk to them, on a normal day, to see how they were getting on. However, on the first of his new style visits he was shocked to find the branch waiting as if it were ready to greet the company's chief executive. The place was spick and span, every desk was clear of paper, and the marks on the wall showed where notices had recently been removed. Everyone was in their best clothes and appeared anxious. The next and the third visits were just the same. Oh dear, thought Steven, what am I going to do to convince them to be normal?

It might have been better if he had explained to the branch managers what he was trying to do. Instead of getting an overreaction from his staff, he would have been able to obtain the support from the very people he needs to be his allies. Rather than being suspicious, if told, they could well have been more tolerant of his attempts to change.

We have already agreed that the learning climate is one in which everyone is allowed to have weaknesses or areas that are in need of improvement. Without those factors, there would be no reason to learn in the first place. Openness and learning are interlinked and interdependent. The manager is crucial to the creation of such a climate. The manager's behaviour, as witnessed by the staff, sets the scene. If you, the boss, are able to declare your learning needs and demonstrate your determination to act, there is a greater chance that your staff will follow suit. Equally, if you are not prepared to make those admissions, why should you expect your staff to do something you are not prepared to do?

Can you imagine how a group of employees would respond in the following situation? The company decided to invest in information technology to modernise its operating, information and communications systems. The plan was for every member of staff to have a PC on their desk. A senior manager, the director of resources, was given responsibility for the implementation of the plan.

Some members of staff were sceptical about the size of the investment, especially as they had recently been told that their annual pay rise was to be below the rate of inflation and the training budget was to be reduced because of the company's poor financial performance. Training in the new system was to be compulsory. This too was greeted with some opposition as it would take away even more resources from the already reduced budget.

The new system was installed and training carried out. The machines were switched on with varying degrees of enthusiasm. Imagine the opponents' glee when the rumours about the director of resource's computer competence began to circulate. His private tuition was the first leak. The second was, despite the special attention he had received, he still couldn't find the on/off switch. Some of the company's jokers tested out the truth. E-mail after e-mail was answered by his secretary and carefully phrased questions at meetings soon revealed his lack of knowledge and experience.

Attendance at the training began to fall off and the old routines scrapped in favour of the computer-based system began to creep back. When the board reviewed the plan's success, a year after implementation, there was a great deal of surprise and dismay at its failure.

It is possible that you too will find some opposition from those who do not understand or the cynics who do not believe the extent of your commitment. Do not be swayed from your determination to change and learn new skills. The take-up curve used in marketing is relevant here. The normal distribution can be applied to your staff just as well as the market for a new product.

Figure 7.9: Marketing distribution

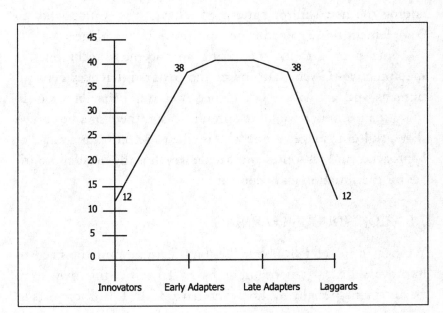

You will find supporters in the *innovators*. They are the people who grasp new ideas with enthusiasm. The *early adapters* come along second. They need to be convinced but quickly adopt the new ideas. Those who need to be convinced by experience are the *late adapters*. The *laggards* will never be convinced, no matter how hard you try. Why waste time and energy on the *laggards* when it should be spent with the *innovators* and *early adapters*? Their experiences will sway the *late adapters*. By then you will have taken over 80 per cent of your workforce with you.

If you are prepared to give support and tolerance to others, you should be equally fair to yourself. It would not be normal to go through a period of learning without experiencing some degree of pain. Starting any new venture is likely to cause some difficulty. Learning, by its very process, will be taking you into areas that you have not encountered before, challenging your existing attitudes and ways of working and exposing you to unfamiliar concepts and practices. It can be dangerous – there is the chance you will not succeed. It is possible that learning will contain some discomfort and even embarrassment. That is the reality of learning. However on the other hand, there is the excitement, the thrill of achievement and the sense of gain. The reward is adding the new skill or pattern of behaviour to your toolkit to complement those gained from your previous experience.

Some people think that using management techniques is manipulative. Given that one of the major differences between humans and animals is our choice over our behaviour, we do more than simply respond to stimuli. It can, therefore, be argued that a skilful manager is one who is able to select from a range of approaches and responses and decide which is the most appropriate for the situation and people in it.

7.5 CONTINUOUS LEARNING

We hear a lot of talk about life-long learning and the need to improve skills on a continuous basis. To some, this may seem exhausting; especially to those who have worked hard for years to gain a qualification. To others, this sort of phrase may seem like bland rhetoric – sounding good but meaning nothing. In fact, it should mean a lot. It is more than just going on endless courses that waste your time, or doing things for the sake of it. Continuous learning is a state of mind and a way of being. It can be hard work; it can also be very enjoyable.

It means seeing each new task and situation as containing the opportunity for learning. It means being open to new ideas and being ready to consider existing ones from other perspectives. It means listening closely to what other people are saying and asking them to explain why they do a task a certain way or why they hold a particular opinion. This can lead to greater appreciation and insight and give you a broader view of the world and introduce you to ideas you might not previously have considered. It can also encourage the other person to question their own assumptions and practices.

Observing how other people behave towards each other is another marvellous way of considering other ways of behaving. Some actions will be very effective and you may wish to add them to your repertoire. Others will have disastrous consequences and you may vow never to behave in that way.

Observing how people react to you also indicates which patterns of behaviour work well or fail in different circumstances. Even if asking them for feedback is not appropriate, you can assess the impact you have had on them. For example, a sense of embarrassment is good indicator of having got something wrong. When something goes well, you might feel a warm glow of satisfaction. Learning how to read your own senses can be part of your personal development plan.

Other aids to continuous learning include the use of a journal or learning diary. A simple notebook will do. In it, you can record your thoughts and lessons as you learn them. Not only will the journal serve as an *aide memoir*, it will help you chart your progress over the years.

Reading and talking about your work with staff and colleagues demonstrates the action. Discussion also helps to share your learning with others and contributes to the development of a culture where learning is normal. As the manager, your role is to take the lead in setting standards and making changes. If you do not demonstrate your commitment to your own development, why should your staff believe that you are serious about theirs? This means making learning and change the central part of your normal working life.

Thus, the first step to take in getting better at managing people's performance is to make sure that you learn how to get better at managing your own. Having made a start perhaps you will want to share your thoughts and experience with others. Building a virtuous learning cycle will pay dividends and create the climate where the people dimension is a positive strength in your management abilities.

BIBLIOGRAPHY

C Chambers, J Coopey & McLean, *Develop Your Management Potential* (London: Kogan Page) 1990.

M Dale, *Developing Management Skills* (London: Kogan Page) 1998.

Drucker, *The Practice of Management* (London: Heron) 1955.

C Handy, *Understanding Organisations* (London: Penguin) 1985.

D A Kolb, *Experiential Learning: Experiences as the Sources of Learning and Development* (Eaglewood Cliffs, NJ: Prentice Hall) 1984.

D McGregor, *The Human Side of Enterprise* (New York: McGraw Hill, 1960.

R Mager, *Goal Analysis* (Belmont: Pitman) 1984.

J G March & H A Simon, *Organisations* (New York: John Wiley) 1958.

A H Maslow, *Motivation and Personality* (New York: Harper) 1954.

E Mayo, *The Social Problems of an Industrial Civilisation* (Cambridge, Mass.: Harvard) 1945.

M Pedler, J Burgoyne & T Boydell, *A Manager's Guide to Self-development* (London: McGraw Hill, 1994.

J Peters & R H Waterman, *In Search of Excellence: Lessons from America's Best-run Companies* (New York: Harper & Row) 1982.